Megan + Dan

Thank you for such an incredible weekend in Montana! It was so special to be apart of this big step of yours. I LOVED getting to meet your family and LOVED how special and personal you made this weekend. Cannot wait to spend the next 100 years with you love birds! Saw this book at a coffee shop in big sky and know how much you both love to cook and we thought it would be fun for you guys to try some of these recipes on our next camping trip!! Love you both

xo Caitlin

Megadan!
I'm so happy for the two of you and I feel honored to celebrate your big day with you both. you make such an incredible couple and I'm so glad you found each other.
Megan, you truly bring out the best in Dan and I'm so lucky to get to call you a friend. Dan, it's been so special watching how you've grown over the years into such an incredible guy :-)
I look forward to many fun adventures with you both. Let's never get old and boring... the best is yet to come. Love, Adrienne

MARKUS SÄMMER

The GREAT OUTDOORS

120 RECIPES FOR ADVENTURE COOKING

gestalten

INTO THE WILDERNESS

Just after the turn of the century, after many stressful years cooking in top Munich restaurants, I took a long break. It was a break from my profession and my regular life; indeed, it was almost a break from civilization itself. It was a kind of sabbatical. My destination was Australia, return date unknown. All I wanted was to get away.

Equipped with a work/travel visa valid for a year, a huge backpack, and boundless curiosity, I flew into Brisbane. Of course, before this trip I had often set up a tent and camped or cooked outside. But measured against the vastness of the Australian outback, I began my travel adventures as a true greenhorn.

Thankfully, nature proved a very good teacher. Bit by bit, the distances I ventured led me further and further away from all civilization, and overnight camping trips became longer and more frequent. I learned to orient myself by the sun, and took my cues from it as to when it was time to start looking for a suitable camping spot for the night, gather firewood, and set up my tent. Making a fire was especially tricky. Oftentimes the risk of fire was great, so I had to find a safe and protected place for it. Gathering firewood was also dangerous. Since poisonous spiders, scorpions, and snakes like to hide in dry wood, it was best to check each branch carefully.

My pile of equipment kept growing, and after a while I bought a station wagon. Before long, it was loaded to the ceiling with surfboards, diving and fishing equipment, and, of course, camping and cooking equipment. Along the way, while surfing or trekking, I would meet really nice people and often invite them to share a meal.

My meals were varied, even sumptuous, thanks to the fish, mussels, and crabs I caught.

Now and then, in exchange for lodging, I also worked for farmers who gave me fabulous fresh fruits and vegetables. This wonderful trip lasted almost a whole year, during which I traveled 24,855 miles (40,000 kilometers), rounding the entire continent along the Australian coast. On countless nights I slept under the open sky. During this journey, I came up with many ideas and recipes that have now found their way into this book.

My most extreme camp cooking experience was definitely in 2011, in Peru, during an eight-week expedition in the Peruvian Andes. There, I frequently had to rustle up nutritious and tasty meals under difficult circumstances for my climbing partner and me. We often had little room for our equipment, and camped at extremely high altitudes. Still, at an altitude of 3,400 miles (5,500 meters), neither the usual cooking techniques nor our appetites were quite the same as at sea level.

Several years have gone by since then, during which I mostly traveled in a Volkswagen camper van between the coasts of the North Sea and the Baltic Sea, South Tyrol, Lake Garda, Sardinia, and Corsica. The idea for this book was conceived during these wanderings.

With this book, I hope to pass on the knowledge and experiences I acquired about camp cooking and the outdoors. In turn, may this knowledge accompany you on your own journeys and help to enrich your culinary experiences.

Healthy food is important, especially after a long and physically tiring day outdoors. There's nothing better than a good meal to recharge those batteries and prepare you for the next adventure.

And now, time to go outdoors! Camp, cook, and enjoy life!

Markus

CONTENTS

AT HOME

14–41   PREPARING FOR YOUR TRIP

QUICK REFUEL

70–101   FAST POWER FOOD

DINING OUT

154–205   COOKING OUTDOORS ON THE
BARBECUE AND THE CAMPFIRE

REFRESH

240–259   THIRST-QUENCHERS AND WAKE-UP DRINKS

WAKE-UP CALL

42-63 ALL FUELED UP WITH ENERGY FOR THE DAY

DINING IN

110-145 COOKING ON ONE OR TWO BURNERS IN THE VAN

SWEET LOVE

210-231 SWEETS AND DESSERTS

Recipe Index 262
General Index 264
Special Thanks 270

BREAK TIME

In each of us there is a trace of the original nomads, hunters, and gatherers who lived in the midst of, and with, nature. The feelings of inner peace, well-being, and the attraction of a campfire are familiar to us all. This has been the case since the beginning of humankind. The longing to rediscover these feelings and to experience them fully is often the reason we campers have the urge to be outside. The magic word is *grounded*—being connected to the earth.

Camping means freedom, independence, experiencing nature, relaxing, and letting one's soul "chill." It also means sticking around in places that simply appeal to us, or in which we can pursue our sport.

From that very first moment, when the camping van is packed and the key turns in the ignition, we are completely in the here and now. The stress of daily life is quickly forgotten. Many times it is simply "the path that is the goal," and it's okay to let oneself drift. Weather and sunlight determine the rhythm. We are carefree and firmly in the moment.

No matter where you end up on that very first morning—at a lake, in the mountains, beside the ocean—the view from the window is always beautiful and much more captivating than any a hotel can offer. At a microcosmic campsite of 32 square feet (3 square meters), little rituals can create enormous happiness: getting the coffee pot ready; its gurgling and hissing; the aroma of a freshly brewed cup; the smell of freedom and adventure.

It is during evenings with friends, when you are carefree, happily cooking and feeling the vibe of togetherness, that camping inspires the same feelings of joy as when you live simply. Every camper knows the exact feeling. When it comes down to it, you need very few material goods to be completely happy and at peace.

BEFORE YOU LEAVE HOME

Unless otherwise indicated, the recipes in this book are designed for two people. Since you won't necessarily have a scale or a measuring cup at hand on a trip, most measurements are given in cups or standard package sizes and other practical units. Quite a few recipes also provide instructions for variations, as well as other tips and tricks. To help you find your way around the recipes, I have assigned them symbols so you can quickly see which recipes are good for the trail, or fast to prepare, or don't need much equipment, and so on.

Practical and quick recipes to fill your lunchbox with food that satiates, gives you energy, and tastes delicious! They are especially geared to providing you with food for the whole day. They just require a bit of preparation.

The feather indicates especially light dishes that also make good snacks. They won't make you feel sleepy—you will remain fit and alert for the rest of the day.

The carrot points to vegetarian dishes and variations. In fact, these recipes are always a good choice, especially if you don't have a cooler for fish or meat and the next market is far away.

Dishes that will fill you up and refuel you with loads of energy, whether enjoyed before or after a long day outside. Pow!

The best part of camp cooking is a warming fire or a sizzling grill. These are great recipes for a cozy evening outside, as well as recipes best prepared outdoors in a skillet or frying pan (so you won't have to endure the smell of fried food in the van for days afterwards).

Are you traveling in a small car, do you not have much equipment, or have you been away trekking for several days with just a tent? The tent icon stands for quick, simple dishes that call for just a few easily transported ingredients and, for the most part, only a stove or a campfire.

If you are pressed for time, this icon will lead you to the right recipes. Even if your stomach is growling and you have to refuel quickly, or if you have very little time to cook, you can whip up something tasty in just a few short steps.

Recipes with this symbol do not require any cooking at all.

Here you can quickly find recipes calling for only one stove.

For these recipes you will need two sources of heat, such as a stove with two burners.

CHECK THE WEATHER!

The weather can turn very quickly, especially in the mountains, and your journey can become very uncomfortable, even dangerous. Don't forget to check the weather report before starting out, and always keep a sharp eye out for changing weather.

AT HOME

PREPARING FOR YOUR TRIP

It's finally time! The new outdoor season has begun. But before setting off, you must pack your camper van properly and get it ready for your trip. Making a list really helps not to lose sight of anything—just check each item off as you pack it. In the following pages, you will find tips and packing lists covering all aspects of your travel kitchen. What to take along and what to leave behind always depends on how long you are planning to be away.

However, you will also find a few recipes you can make ahead, in preparation for your trip. For example, try baking your own hamburger buns at home and discover a world of difference. You will definitely look forward to having a burger!

KITCHEN EQUIPMENT

STAPLES

HERBS AND SPICES

ALWAYS
ON
BOARD

KITCHEN EQUIPMENT CHECKLIST:
- [ ] Bottle opener/corkscrew
- [ ] Bowls and storage containers
- [ ] Camp stove (two are best), and fuel such as propane gas, gas, or petroleum fuel
- [ ] Campfire equipment (a folding saw; an axe; wood, possibly; fire starters, perhaps DIY)
- [ ] Can opener
- [ ] Cooking utensils (spatulas, cooking spoons, whisks, etc.)
- [ ] Cutlery
- [ ] Cutting board
- [ ] Dishes (plates, bowls, cups, etc.)
- [ ] Dishwashing bowl containing a sponge, a dishcloth, and dish soap
- [ ] Frying pans; pots; a sieve with a strong handle
- [ ] Garbage bags
- [ ] Glasses/tumblers
- [ ] Glass jar with a sprouting lid
- [ ] Grater
- [ ] Grill (charcoal; lighter or matches; tongs; glove)
- [ ] Hand mixer (optional)
- [ ] Headlamp; flashlights
- [ ] Knives (2-3 large ones; some folding ones)
- [ ] Lighter; matches
- [ ] Lunchbox
- [ ] Paper towel rolls
- [ ] Plastic food storage bags
- [ ] Rubber bands
- [ ] Storage container (for food, leftovers, etc.)
- [ ] Tealight candles
- [ ] Vegetable peeler
- [ ] Water container or a prefilled water tank
- [ ] Wood or metal skewers

HERB AND SPICE CHECKLIST:
- [ ] Chilies, dried
- [ ] Oregano, dried
- [ ] Pepper, black, in a pepper mill
- [ ] Ras el hanout (Moroccan spice mix)
- [ ] Sea salt
- [ ] Turmeric, ground

STAPLES CHECKLIST:
- [ ] Capers
- [ ] Coconut milk
- [ ] Eggs
- [ ] Garlic
- [ ] Ginger, fresh or powdered
- [ ] Honey, liquid
- [ ] Hot sauce (such as sriracha)
- [ ] Milk, ultra-pasteurized
- [ ] Mustard (such as Dijon)
- [ ] Olive oil; canola oil (both cold-pressed)
- [ ] Olives
- [ ] Onions
- [ ] Parmesan cheese, piece
- [ ] Pasta (such as light spelt penne or spaghetti)
- [ ] Rice (long-grain, such as basmati or jasmine, and risotto rice, such as arborio)
- [ ] Soy sauce
- [ ] Sugar, brown or coconut
- [ ] Tomato paste
- [ ] Tomatoes, canned
- [ ] Tuna, canned (or other fish, such as salmon or mackerel)
- [ ] Vegetable stock, organic
- [ ] Vinegar, balsamic

BURGER BUNS

½ CUP (130 ML) MILK
1 TBSP SUGAR
¾ OZ (20 G) FRESH YEAST
OR 1¾ TSP (3.5 G) INSTANT YEAST
2 TBSP UNSALTED BUTTER, MELTED
2 CUPS (250 G) ALL-PURPOSE FLOUR
OR LIGHT SPELT FLOUR
½ TSP SALT
2 EGGS AT ROOM TEMPERATURE
2 TBSP WHITE SESAME SEEDS

Make a starter: stir together the milk, sugar, yeast, and butter until foamy. Preheat the oven to 375 °F (190 °C).

In a large bowl, mix together the flour and salt. Add 1 egg and the starter, and knead to make a dough. The dough should be neither too sticky nor too firm; work in a bit more flour or milk as needed. Cover the dough and let it rise for 1 hour. Knead the dough to remove air bubbles, and shape it into 6 flat buns. Cover the buns and let them rise for 30 minutes.

Whisk the remaining egg with about 1 tablespoon of water. Brush the egg wash over the buns, and sprinkle with sesame seeds. Bake for 20 minutes or until golden brown. Remove buns from the oven, and set aside to cool covered with a kitchen towel to keep them soft. The buns can be frozen in a freezer bag, or just taken along with you.

BASIC PESTO RECIPE

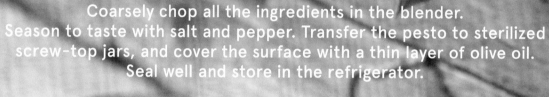

Coarsely chop all the ingredients in the blender.
Season to taste with salt and pepper. Transfer the pesto to sterilized
screw-top jars, and cover the surface with a thin layer of olive oil.
Seal well and store in the refrigerator.

SUN-DRIED TOMATO PESTO

½ BUNCH BASIL
5 ½ OZ (150 G) SUN-DRIED TOMATOES
1 ¾ OZ (50 G) HARD CHEESE, SUCH AS PARMESAN
1 OZ (30 G) PINE NUTS OR OTHER NUTS
1 GARLIC CLOVE
1 SMALL RED CHILI PEPPER
2 TBSP TOMATO PASTE
⅔ CUP (150 ML) OLIVE OIL
SEA SALT AND BLACK PEPPER

Pick basil leaves from the stems, wash them, and shake them dry (discard stems).
Using kitchen shears, cut the tomatoes into strips. Coarsely grate the cheese.
In a dry skillet, lightly toast the nuts. Peel and crush the garlic. Deseed and thinly slice the chili pepper. Proceed with the basic pesto recipe.

PESTO GENOVESE

1 BUNCH BASIL
1 ¾ OZ (50 G) HARD CHEESE,
SUCH AS PARMESAN
1 OZ (30 G) PINE NUTS
1 GARLIC CLOVE
⅔ CUP (150 ML) OLIVE OIL
SALT AND BLACK PEPPER

Pick basil leaves from the stems, wash them, and shake them dry (discard stems).
Coarsely grate the cheese. In a dry skillet, lightly toast the pine nuts.
Peel and crush the garlic.
Proceed with the basic pesto recipe.

WILD GARLIC PESTO

1 BUNCH WILD GARLIC OR RAMPS
1 ¾ OZ (50 G) HARD CHEESE
1 OZ (30 G) PINE NUTS OR OTHER NUTS
⅔ CUP (150 ML) OLIVE OIL
ZEST OF 1 ORGANIC LEMON
SALT AND BLACK PEPPER
CHILI FLAKES (OPTIONAL)

Wash and trim the wild garlic, and roughly cut it up using kitchen shears.
Coarsely grate the cheese.
In a dry skillet, lightly toast the pine nuts.
Proceed with the basic pesto recipe.

BEETROOT PESTO

1 BEET
1 ¾ OZ (50 G) HARD CHEESE,
SUCH AS AGED GOAT CHEESE
1 OZ (30 G) WALNUTS
⅔ CUP (150 ML) OLIVE OIL
SALT AND BLACK PEPPER

Wrap the beet in aluminum foil.
Place in the the oven and bake at 350 °F (180 °C) for 40 minutes. When slightly cool, peel and roughly cut the beet into pieces. Coarsely grate the cheese. In a dry skillet, lightly toast the walnuts. Proceed with the basic pesto recipe.

TIP:
Beetroot pesto can be refined by adding the seeds
of half a vanilla bean and a sprinkle of chili flakes.

SYRUP

You can concoct wonderfully fresh-tasting cold drinks, hot drinks, cocktails, and mixed drinks from syrups. Recipes for these drinks can be found in the "Refresh" chapter (page 240).
First, you always make a simple syrup by boiling water and sugar together, then adding other ingredients. For a more concentrated flavor, let the syrup stand in a cool place for several hours or overnight. Strain the syrup through a sieve, and transfer to sterilized bottles while still hot. (The syrup will last even longer if you boil it again briefly after straining it.) Seal the bottles immediately. To help extend its shelf life, for every 4 cups of syrup you can add 2 tablespoons of ascorbic acid (vitamin C, available in drugstores or health food stores). Alternatively, you can use citric acid (usually found in the baking aisle of grocery stores), but follow the instructions on the package.

RHUBARB SYRUP

4 CUPS WATER, 1 LB 2 OZ (500 G) SUGAR, 1 LB 2 OZ (500 G) RHUBARB, JUICE OF 1 LEMON, 2 APPLES

Wash, peel, and cut the rhubarb into small pieces. Wash, core, and dice the apples. Place all ingredients in a pot and simmer, uncovered, for 15 minutes.

ELDERFLOWER SYRUP

4 CUPS WATER, 1 LB 2 OZ (500 G) SUGAR, 15–20 FRESH OR 10 DRIED ELDERFLOWER BLOSSOMS, JUICE OF 3 LEMONS

Place the water and the sugar in a pot and bring to a boil. While the syrup is still hot, add the elderflower blossoms and the lemon juice. Let steep overnight.

CHAI SYRUP

4 CUPS WATER, 1 LB 10 OZ (750 G) BROWN SUGAR, 2 CINNAMON STICKS, 5 TBSP FENNEL SEEDS, 2 TBSP WHOLE CLOVES, 2 TBSP CARDAMOM PODS, 4 STAR ANISE, ¼ OZ (10 G) FRESH GINGER

Split the cinnamon sticks. Using a mortar and pestle, coarsely grind the fennel seeds, cloves, cardamom, and star anise.
Peel and finely chop the ginger.
Place all ingredients in a pot and simmer, uncovered, for 15 minutes. Let steep for 1 hour.

GINGER SYRUP

4 CUPS WATER, 1 LB 2 OZ (500 G) SUGAR, 10 OZ (300 G) FRESH GINGER, JUICE OF 2 LIMES

Peel and finely chop the ginger.
Place all ingredients in a pot and simmer, uncovered, for 10 minutes.

HOMEMADE
PRESERVES

STRAWBERRY AND RHUBARB JAM

1 LB 2 OZ (500 G) RHUBARB, 1 LB 2 OZ (500 G) STRAWBERRIES, 1 VANILLA BEAN, 1 ORGANIC LEMON, 1 LB 2 OZ (500 G) GELLING SUGAR 2:1 (SEE NOTE)

Peel the rhubarb, hull the strawberries, and cut them both into small pieces. Split the vanilla bean, scrape out the seeds, then cut the bean in half crosswise. Wash the lemon in hot water, zest it, and juice it. Place the rhubarb, strawberries, vanilla seeds, vanilla bean halves, lemon zest, and lemon juice in a pot. Add the sugar. Bring to a vigorous boil and cook for 3 minutes, stirring constantly. Transfer the jam into sterilized jars while still hot, leaving a ¼ inch (5 mm) headspace. Seal immediately.

Note: Gelling sugar is available online. If you cannot source it, use regular sugar and light pectin crystals instead, and follow the instructions on the package.

CARAMELIZED PLUM COMPOTE

2 LB 2 OZ (1 KG) PLUMS, 5 ½ OZ (150 G) SUGAR, 1 CINNAMON STICK, 4 TSP (2 CL) RUM OR TO TASTE

Halve and pit the plums. In a pot, heat the sugar without stirring it, until it caramelizes and turns a light brown. Add the plums and the cinnamon stick, bring to a boil, and stir until the sugar has dissolved again. Stir in the rum. Remove the cinnamon stick and pour the compote into sterilized jars while still hot, leaving a ¼ inch (5 mm) headspace. Seal immediately. The compote tastes fabulous with Imperial Pancakes (page 225).

TYROLEAN NUT CAKES BAKED IN JARS

6 EGGS
7 OZ (200 G) LIGHT CANE SUGAR
PINCH OF SALT
7 OZ (200 G) UNSALTED BUTTER
7 OZ (200 G) GROUND HAZELNUTS
4 ½ OZ (125 G) ALL-PURPOSE FLOUR
1 TSP BAKING POWDER
1 TSP CINNAMON
3 ½ OZ (100 G) RAISINS,
BRIEFLY BOILED IN 4 TSP (2 CL)
RUM AND 1 TSP WATER
ZEST OF ½ ORGANIC LEMON
7 OZ (200 G) GRATED DARK CHOCOLATE
COOKING SPRAY OR VEGETABLE OIL

Preheat a convection oven to 325 °F (160 °C) or a conventional oven to 350 °F (180 °C).

Separate the eggs. Beat the egg whites with a bit of sugar and a pinch of salt until stiff peaks form. In a separate bowl, beat the egg yolks with the remaining sugar until foamy. Stir in the nuts, flour, baking powder, cinnamon, raisins, and lemon zest. Carefully fold in the beaten egg whites and grated chocolate.

Grease the inside of clean jars with a bit of oil or cooking spray. Fill the jars two-thirds full with batter. Bake for 25-30 minutes, or until a toothpick inserted into the center comes out clean; the smaller the jars, the shorter the baking time. As soon as the cakes are done, using oven mitts, seal the jars with the lids. Be careful, the jars will be very hot! To serve, invert the cakes onto a plate and slice.

Refrigerated, the cakes will keep for at least four weeks.

HOMEMADE GRANOLA AND PORRIDGE MIXES

Prepared at home before you leave and stored in a dry place, granola and other such mixes keep for a long time and provide valuable energy. To save weight and space, it is best to store granola in ziplock bags.

BREAKFAST PORRIDGE

9 OZ (250 G) CEREAL FLAKES (ROLLED OATS, ROLLED SPELT, OR ROLLED MULTIGRAIN FLAKES) GROUND NUTS, SEEDS, ALMONDS, COCONUT FLOUR, CINNAMON, GROUND VANILLA, PUFFED AMARANTH (AS DESIRED)

In a food processor, coarsely chop the cereal. Mix in your preferred combination of nuts, seeds, and spices, and store mix in an airtight container. This mix makes a quick and super simple breakfast when you are on the road.

Preparation:
In a bowl, place about ½ cup of cereal mix for each serving. Add hot water or hot milk, stir, and let the grains absorb the liquid for a few minutes. Enhance the flavor by adding, for example, sugar, honey, agave syrup, cocoa powder, fruits (dried, fresh, frozen,

FUNKY FRUIT

2 TBSP HAZELNUTS
2 TBSP ALMONDS
2 TBSP GROUND FLAXSEED
2 TBSP WHITE SESAME SEEDS
10 OZ (300 G) MIXED CEREAL FLAKES,
SUCH AS OATS OR SPELT
2 TBSP CANOLA OR SUNFLOWER OIL
PINCH OF SALT
2 TBSP HONEY
½ TSP CINNAMON
1 OZ (30 G) FREEZE-DRIED FRUIT

Preheat oven to 340 °F (170 °C).
Coarsely chop the hazelnuts and almonds,
and mix them with all other ingredients
except the fruit. Line a baking sheet with
parchment paper and spread the mixture evenly.
Bake until golden brown, turning the mixture
every 5 minutes. Let cool, then stir in the
dried fruit. Store in an airtight container.

BERRY BOOSTER

2 TBSP HAZELNUTS
2 TBSP ALMONDS
1 OZ (30 G) FREEZE-DRIED BERRIES
1 ¾ OZ (50 G) PUFFED AMARANTH
1 ¾ OZ (50 G) PUFFED QUINOA
3 ½ OZ (100 G) QUICK OATS
3 ½ OZ (100 G) ROLLED SPELT FLAKES
2 TBSP COCONUT CHIPS
2 TBSP WHITE CHOCOLATE CHIPS OR DROPS
(OMIT IF TRAVELING TO HOT AREAS)
6 TBSP CHIA SEEDS

Preheat oven to 340 °F (170 °C).
Coarsely chop the nuts and almonds.
Mix together all ingredients except the fruit.
Line a baking sheet with parchment paper and
spread the mixture evenly. Bake until golden
brown, turning the mixture every 5 minutes.
Let cool, then stir in the dried berries.
Store in an airtight container.

SQUASH COOKIES

3 ½ OZ (100 G) SQUASH
(HOKKAIDO OR BUTTERNUT),
SEEDS REMOVED
1 ¾ OZ (50 G) COCONUT OIL
4 TBSP HONEY
2 EGGS
1 ¾ OZ (50 G) GROUND FLAXSEED
3 OZ (80 G) LIGHTLY ROASTED PUMPKIN SEEDS
4 OZ (120 G) QUICK OATS
4 OZ (120 G) ROLLED OATS
3 OZ (80 G) DRIED CRANBERRIES
OR GOJI BERRIES
½ TSP SALT
1 TSP FINELY CHOPPED FRESH GINGER
PINCH OF CINNAMON
PINCH OF NUTMEG

Preheat oven to 350 °F (180 °C). Dice the squash and boil it in a small amount of water.
When cooked through, drain and purée the squash.

Heat the coconut oil and dissolve the honey into it. In a separate bowl, whisk the eggs.
Transfer all the ingredients to a bowl and mix to combine. Shape the dough into 20 cookies (see tip). Line a baking sheet with parchment paper and arrange the cookies on it.
Bake for 15–20 minutes or until golden brown.

Let cookies cool completely before gently placing them in an airtight storage container.

TIP:
Use a teaspoon to portion the dough.
Press down on each cookie to make rounds about ¾ inch (2 cm) thick.

TRAIL BARS

3 ½ OZ (100 G) DRIED SOFT FIGS
1 ¾ OZ (50 G) DRIED SOFT APRICOTS
3 ½ OZ (100 G) RAISINS
1 ¾ OZ (50 G) HAZELNUTS
1 ¾ OZ (50 G) PUMPKIN SEEDS
1 ¾ OZ (50 G) SUNFLOWER SEEDS
2 APPLES
5 ½ OZ (150 G) SPELT OR
WHOLE WHEAT FLOUR
1 CUP (250 ML) WATER
5 ½ OZ (150 G) QUICK OATS
1 TBSP HONEY
1 TSP CINNAMON
½ TSP SALT
4 TBSP COLD-PRESSED
CANOLA OIL

Preheat oven to 350 °F (180 °C). In a dry skillet, toast nuts and seeds until fragrant, then coarsely chop them. Cut the figs and apricots into bite-sized pieces. Peel and coarsely grate the apples. Place all ingredients in a bowl and knead to combine. Line a baking tray with parchment paper. Spread the mixture evenly over the tray. Bake for about 30 minutes. Let cool a bit, then cut into bars while still slightly warm using a sharp knife. Let cut bars cool completely and allow them to dry for a day, then store in an airtight container.
Use parchment paper to separate the layers so the bars don't stick to each other.

You can substitute other kinds of nuts, seeds, and dried fruit for the ones listed in the recipe, as long you keep the same proportions. Adding shredded coconut will further enhance the flavor of the bars.

TIP:

You can also bake the bar mixture between thin oblaten wafers to make wafer "sandwich" bars.

TRAIL MIXES

MONKEY MUNCH

3 OZ (80 G) SLIVERED ALMONDS
3 OZ (80 G) BANANA CHIPS
3 OZ (80 G) LIGHTLY SALTED PEANUTS
1½ OZ (40 G) DRIED MANGO
1½ OZ (40 G) RAISINS
1 OZ (30 G) COCONUT CHIPS

Thinly slice the mango.
Coarsely chop the banana chips.
Mix all ingredients together
and store in an airtight container.

POWER PUSH

1 ¾ OZ (50 G) DRIED SOFT APRICOTS
1 ¾ OZ (50 G) DRIED SOFT FIGS
1 ¾ OZ (50 G) DRIED GOJI BERRIES
1 ½ OZ (40 G) WALNUTS
1 ½ OZ (40 G) WHOLE BLANCHED ALMONDS
1 ½ OZ (40 G) PUMPKIN SEEDS

Cut the apricots and figs into bite-sized pieces. Coarsely chop the walnuts and almonds. (If you wish, before chopping, you can dry-roast the walnuts, almonds, and pumpkin seeds in the oven.) Mix all ingredients together and store in an airtight container.

MACADAMIA MONSTER

3 OZ (80 G) MACADAMIA NUTS
1 ½ OZ (40 G) HAZELNUTS
1 ½ OZ (40 G) CASHEWS
1 ½ OZ (40 G) DRIED CRANBERRIES
2 OZ (60 G) SOFT DATES

Coarsely chop the nuts. Cut the dates into small pieces. Mix all ingredients together and store in an airtight container.

POWER BALLS
FIG AND NUT BALLS

MAKES 20 BALLS

2 ¾ OZ (75 G) MIXED NUTS AND SEEDS,
SUCH AS HAZELNUTS, CASHEWS, ALMONDS,
OR SUNFLOWER SEEDS
3 ½ OZ (100 G) DRIED SOFT FIGS
4 TBSP (50 G) UNSALTED BUTTER
OR COCONUT OIL
2 TBSP AGAVE SYRUP
OR SUGAR BEET SYRUP
2 TBSP QUICK OATS
2 TBSP PUFFED AMARANTH
TOASTED SESAME SEEDS
OR CHOPPED ALMONDS, FOR COATING

With a knife or in a food processor, chop the nuts. Lightly toast the nuts in a dry skillet. Remove the nuts from the skillet as soon as they start to brown, and let cool. Chop the figs.

Combine the butter or coconut oil and the syrup, and briefly heat together. Add the remaining ingredients and mix well. Remove from the heat and let cool. Shape the mixture into walnut-sized balls, and roll in toasted sesame seeds or chopped almonds to coat. Let balls cool until firm, about 30 minutes. Store in an airtight container, using parchment or wax paper to separate the layers.

APRICOT AND
COCONUT BALLS

FIG AND NUT
BALLS

APRICOT AND COCONUT BALLS

MAKES 20 BALLS

7 OZ (200 G) DRIED SOFT APRICOTS
3 TBSP QUICK OATS
10 TBSP SHREDDED COCONUT,
PLUS EXTRA FOR COATING
2 TBSP AGAVE SYRUP OR
SUGAR BEET SYRUP
1–2 TBSP COCONUT OIL

Finely chop the apricots.

Lightly toast the oats and 5 tablespoons of the shredded coconut in a dry skillet. Add the syrup and the coconut oil to the skillet until heated through. Remove the skillet from the heat.

Stir in the remaining coconut and the chopped apricots. Let the mixture cool. Moisten your hands with water, and shape the mixture into walnut-sized balls. Roll the balls in shredded coconut to coat, and let cool until firm, about 30 minutes. Store the balls in an airtight container, using parchment or wax paper to separate the layers.

WAKE-UP CALL

ALL FUELED UP WITH ENERGY FOR THE DAY

Is there anything more beautiful than waking up in the
midst of nature? I love being the first to open the sliding door
in the morning and squint into the sun, and then,
all sleepy eyes and messy hair, putting the coffee pot on the
stove. The aroma of brewing coffee alone is enough to
perk me up. The lapping of the ocean waves, the fresh wind
coming in from the mountains, the complete stillness of being
alone—when you camp, each new day greets you in a whole
different way. And now, time for a hearty, healthy breakfast in
nature's embrace, to awaken your spirit and fuel your body for a
long, active day in the great outdoors.

A LEGAL HIGH

SUPER GRANOLA

Eating this granola is like being legally doped.
You will feel full, fit, exuberant, and ready to take on any
challenge during a long day outdoors. I love it!

1 CUP FUNKY FRUIT OR
BERRY BOOSTER GRANOLA (PAGE 35)
½ CUP MILK
⅓ CUP FRESH FRUIT SALAD
⅔ CUP (150 G) PLAIN GREEK YOGURT
2 TBSP HONEY OR AGAVE SYRUP

Divide the granola among two bowls or
widemouthed glass jars. Stir in the milk
and the fruit salad. Mix the yogurt
with the honey or agave syrup, and top each
granola bowl with a generous dollop.

PORRIDGE with BANANAS

Porridge and overnight oats are having a moment right now with sports professionals, and they are part of quite a few diet plans. And for good reason! Oats are delicious, easy to digest, and sure to provide you with an abundance of energy for the rest of the day.

½ CUP QUICK OATS
½ CUP MILK, ALMOND MILK, OR OAT MILK
½ CUP WATER
3 TBSP CHAI SYRUP (PAGE 28) OR 2 TBSP HONEY
1 LARGE BANANA
FRESH FIGS AND COCONUT CHIPS (OPTIONAL)

Place the oats, milk, and water into a saucepan and bring to a boil. Simmer for 5-10 minutes. Stir in the chai syrup or honey.

Top the porridge with sliced bananas and figs, if using, and garnish with coconut chips.

OVERNIGHT OATS

3 TBSP CHOPPED DRIED FRUITS, SUCH AS APRICOTS AND DATES
¾ CUP ROLLED OATS
2 CUPS MILK, ALMOND MILK, OR OAT MILK
1 TBSP CHIA SEEDS (OPTIONAL)
2 TBSP HONEY OR AGAVE SYRUP
⅔ CUP (150 G) YOGURT
1 CUP FRESH FRUIT SALAD

In a bowl, place the oats, milk, and chia seeds, if using. Add 1 tablespoon of the honey, stir to combine, and let the oat mixture soak in the refrigerator overnight.

The next morning, divide the oats among two bowls, cups, or wide-mouthed glass jars. To serve, top with the yogurt and dried fruits, and drizzle with the remaining tablespoon of honey.

RICE PUDDING

1 CUP SHORT-GRAIN RICE
4 CUPS MILK
2 TBSP RAW CANE SUGAR, HONEY,
OR AGAVE SYRUP
1 TBSP UNSALTED BUTTER
1 TSP PURE VANILLA EXTRACT (OPTIONAL)
GROUND CINNAMON

Melt the butter in a pot. Add the rice and sauté briefly in the butter. Add the milk, sugar, honey, or syrup, and the vanilla extract, if using. Simmer, stirring constantly and scraping the bottom of the pot so that nothing sticks.

Cover the pot and simmer the rice over the lowest heat setting for 25-30 minutes (or follow the instructions on the package). Stir the rice thoroughly about halfway through the cooking time.

Rice pudding tastes good both warm and cold. If not eating it right away, you might have to add some extra milk to the pudding before serving, since the rice will continue to absorb liquid as it cools. Serve with your choice of toppings.

SUGGESTED TOPPINGS:

Strawberry and rhubarb jam (page 31)
Caramelized plum compote (page 31)
Fresh mango, pineapple, and shredded coconut
Four tablespoons of Power Push trail mix (page 39),
briefly boiled together with 1 tablespoon of honey and 2 tablespoons of water
Fresh berries, diced mixed fruits, apples
(diced and briefly stewed with cinnamon and 1 teaspoon raw cane
sugar or honey), and a few nuts—extremely delicious!

Andes Quinoa Breakfast

I developed this breakfast idea while mountain climbing in Peru. It's terrific, and extremely healthy... but not easy to make at 19,685 ft (6,000 m). At that altitude, quinoa takes, quite literally, forever to cook.

½ CUP QUINOA
½ TSP CINNAMON
2 TBSP RAISINS
1 CUP MILK, ALMOND MILK,
OR OAT MILK
1 APPLE, PLUS ADDITIONAL
APPLE SLICES FOR TOPPING
2 TBSP HONEY
WALNUTS

Place the quinoa, cinnamon, and raisins in a pot and stir to combine. Add the milk, cover the pot, and bring to a gentle boil. Cook over low heat for 10-12 minutes, stirring occasionally. If the milk is fully absorbed before the end of the cooking time, add a few tablespoons of water. Turn off the heat and let the porridge stand for 5 minutes.

Grate the apple and add it to the porridge. Stir in the honey. Garnish with extra apple slices and walnuts, and serve.

MY DREAM MOUNTAIN—ALPAMAYO

Excerpts from my Peru expedition journal

DAY 37

August 17, 2011, 8:00 a.m. The taxi is a half-hour late picking me up. Today we're setting off towards Alpamayo and Quitaraju.
But first, we have to go to Sergio's office. It's chaos. Then, back to the guesthouse to pick up the dry food and all our other purchases. We stop again in Caraz. Using the rest of my cash, we stock up on supplies for the coming week. All I have left is 10 centimos, but, at 19,685 ft (6,000 m), there's nothing you can buy anyway. We are late, and only reach Cashapampa, our starting point for the Santa Cruz Valley, in the midday heat. More stress loading the donkeys (they transport the heavy equipment up to base camp). When we finally strike out at 9,678 ft (2,950 m), it's already afternoon. The deep gorge, with its high cliffs towering over us, is extremely hot. Drenched in sweat, we feel like salty pretzels being baked in an oven as we wheeze our way upward. But the gorge is beautiful. Below, a crystal-clear, gurgling river winds its way alongside our path, cacti and azaleas all around. The trees are covered with epiphytic bromeliads in search of light; the climate here is much warmer than in the Ishinca gorge. By the time we finally reach our first campground, we have climbed a total of 2,624 ft (800 m) in altitude, hiked about 6 miles (10 km), and now find ourselves at 12,303 ft (3,750 m). Stomachs growling, we wait for the donkeys to arrive with our equipment. When they finally do, it's already getting dark. Quickly we set up the tents, only to discover that, frustratingly, one of our two tents can no longer be used for the high camp. I prepare an improvised dinner, and we retreat into the other tent.

DAY 38

We break camp after breakfast, and start off around 9:00 a.m. in the direction of base camp. The sweeping Santa Cruz valley, which is relatively flat, lies before us. We come upon a marshy landscape, reminiscent of Africa, covered by a beautiful, shimmering turquoise lagoon. Not much further, we leave the main valley and turn into a smaller one that climbs ever steeper. One more hour later, we come to the Alpamayo base camp at 14,272 ft (4,350 m). Clouds are increasing, and they constantly give off drops of rain. Apparently, the Summit Club, with a 12-person trekking team, has already struck camp in the next-highest camp, the Moraine Camp. Tomorrow, we want to pass this camp and forge on immediately, climbing until we reach high camp. We won't be running into any more trekkers there. Hopefully the weather will improve by midday tomorrow, along with the gurgling in my stomach!

ALPAMAYO—MY DREAM MOUNTAIN

DAY 39

I will need all my strength today. I leave base
camp about 7:30 a.m., along with my heavy 55 lb
(25 kg) backpack, and head in the direction
of Campo 1. The donkeys stay behind since
they won't be able to carry loads across this
terrain. Today, the sun shows itself again,
and it warms me as I am climbing. I soon have a
great view of a massive lagoon, into which
a large glacier is calving. Blas comes up to
join me and we pass Moraine Camp. At about
16,732 ft (5,100 m), after much tortuous rock
balancing, the glacier begins. We rope up.
Traversing the ever-steeper terrain with a heavy
backpack costs me an unbelievable amount of
energy. My back and hips hurt; my thighs burn
under the burden. Finally, at about 18,209 ft
(5,550 m) we gain the col, and we make a
short descent down the other side to the high
camp, which lies at 18,045 ft (5,500 m).
After seven hours, during which I climbed a
total of 3,937 ft (1,200 m) in altitude
with a heavy pack, I am utterly bone-tired and
unsure whether I can summon the energy for
the climb to the summit of Alpamayo.
Now to set up the tent, sort out the climbing
equipment, eat, and go to sleep quickly.

51

The alarm clock jolts me awake at 1:30 a.m.
It hailed during the night, and it is cold and
cloudy. Around 2:15 a.m. we climb by the light
of our headlamps towards the crevasse. When we
reach it, we also reach the first crux: there
is a good 33 feet (10m) of steep, fluted ice to
overcome, followed by a tricky crossing over a
tiny ledge above a deep crevasse.

Now we are in the gully of "French Direct."
Though a steeper and more demanding route than
"Ferrari," it is still safer. Unfortunately,
the weather is really not helping me climb my
dream mountain. In the thick fog and clouds
surrounding us, the rope disappears high up
into nothingness. I can hardly make out anything
beneath me, which really helps minimize the
feeling of complete helplessness. On the first
pitch after the crevasse, we make swift progress
upward through a gully about 70 degrees steep
and filled with very hard firn. Eventually the
snow turns into sheer ice, brittle and hard
as glass. Placing the ice tools properly is
draining, and the crampons need a pretty hard
kick to fasten securely, too. In contrast,
anchoring gives us few problems. We can usually
place the ice screws perfectly in the hard ice.
We are fully focused on the here and now.

On the sixth pitch, the terrain steepens.
We climb along an 80-degree slope in a narrowing
gully. Brief openings in the clouds allow me to
glimpse all the way down to high camp, which is
at least 1,312ft (400m) below us. This feels
more like serious Russian winter climbing.
I am happy with my shoes, which have two layers.
I'm wearing two pairs of socks, but still get
cold toes when anchoring. My fingers freeze.
At these altitudes, it is a truly uncomfortable—
and unbelievably exhausting—night climb.

As the day slowly breaks, the gray cones of
light cast by our headlamps give way to even
grayer daylight.

Two more pitches later, we finally reach
the summit around 8:00 a.m. I don't really
experience an intense feeling of happiness; it
doesn't quite come this time around. The last
two days have cost me a great deal of energy.
Even so, here we are, standing atop my dream
peak. Our rope team will be the only team to
successfully summit Alpamayo for a week; yet
our stay on the summit, which is about 19,685ft

(6,000m) high, is brief. There's just time
enough for a handful of photos, a sip of tea,
and a solidly-frozen trail bar. Then we begin
to rappel down. This is the absolute best part
of the day. It isn't a strenuous descent but,
even so, we need total focus. We conscientiously
check the anchors already fixed in the ice
tunnels, and our slings, too. Despite our
fatigue, there is no room for error when tying
into the ropes and belaying each other.

We reach camp at 10:30 a.m. It took eight hours
to complete the route: six for the climb, two
for rappelling and down-climbing. Our time
wasn't bad. Unfortunately, the weather has not
improved, so it's time for a siesta.
No matter—I am so thankful for gaining the
summit and returning safely. These were the
most strenuous twenty-four hours I have ever
experienced while mountain climbing. The emotions
I experienced after the successful climb will
wash over me only days afterwards. The question
of why people place themselves in such borderline
situations is simple to answer. You feel
yourself, your whole being. You push your limits.
You set your mind on a goal. Whether or not you
succeed is of no consequence; the mere fact that
you've tried has made it all worthwhile.

SUPER FRIED EGGS

1 TBSP CANOLA OIL
6 CHERRY TOMATOES
2 LEEKS
4 EGGS
HOT SAUCE, SUCH AS SRIRACHA,
OR 1 RED CHILI PEPPER
SALT AND BLACK PEPPER
FRESHLY CHOPPED MIXED HERBS
OLIVES, ARUGULA,
SPINACH, SMOKED BACON,
PROSCIUTTO (OPTIONAL)

In a skillet, heat the oil. Halve the cherry tomatoes. Slice the leeks. Add both to the skillet, sauté them briefly, and break the eggs on top. Reduce the heat and season to taste with salt, pepper, and hot sauce. (If using a fresh chili pepper instead, seed it, slice it, and sauté it together with the tomatoes and the leeks.) Sprinkle with the herbs and serve, or top with your choice of olives, arugula, spinach, and smoked bacon or prosciutto.

If you have a sprouting jar in your camper, sprouts are perfect with this dish.

4 MINUTE TEA EGGS

2-4 EGGS
ENOUGH WATER TO COVER
EGGS IN A SINGLE LAYER
2 TEA BAGS

Using a pin or thumbtack, prick a tiny hole in the base of the eggs. Place them in a saucepan with the cold water. Cover the saucepan and bring to a boil. When the water starts to boil, turn off the heat immediately, add the tea bags to the water, cover the saucepan, and set your timer for 4 minutes.

When the timer goes off, remove the eggs and tea bags from the saucepan, and enjoy your tea and perfect soft-boiled eggs while still hot.

This method saves time, fuel, and water!

WESTERN BREAKFAST

This is a really classic dish that will make your heart beat faster whether or not you are a fan of Westerns. It's a power boost for a day full of action, and it gives you everything you need to recharge your batteries before setting off. Yee-haw, be two-wheeled cowboys and cowgirls for the day!

14 OZ (400 G) CANNED BAKED BEANS
CHILI POWDER
4–6 SLICES OF BACON
2 TBSP CANOLA OIL
4 EGGS
1 SWEET POTATO
1 ORGANIC ORANGE
2 TBSP MAPLE SYRUP
SALT AND BLACK PEPPER

In a saucepan, warm the beans over low heat. Season to taste with chili powder, salt and pepper, and set aside.

In a skillet, add 1 tablespoon of the oil and the bacon, and fry until crisp. Break the eggs over the bacon and cook until the yolk is just set. The bacon will be salty enough, so season only with pepper.

And now to refine this classic breakfast dish: Peel and grate the sweet potato. Wash the orange in hot water and zest it. Mix the potato and orange zest with the maple syrup, and add salt and pepper to taste. In another skillet, heat the remaining tablespoon of oil and add the potato mixture; you can shape it into a pancake or fry it as a hash. Fry on both sides until golden brown. If you like, peel the orange to eat later.

TIP

Instead of canned baked beans you can use canned kidney beans. Drain the beans, stir in 2 tablespoons of tomato paste and a bit of water, and heat.

EVERY DAY OUTDOORS
RESTORES THE SOUL!

POWER FRITTATA WITH OATS

Unlike a regular omelet, this frittata delivers long-lasting energy thanks to the oats. It makes you feel full for a long time, not to mention it tastes great.

1 TOMATO
4 EGGS
½ CUP QUICK OATS
HANDFUL OF FRESHLY CHOPPED MIXED HERBS, OR BABY SPINACH AND CRUMBLED FETA CHEESE
SALT AND BLACK PEPPER
CANOLA OIL, FOR FRYING
2 BAGELS OR WHOLEGRAIN BREAD ROLLS
½ SERVING AVOCADO DIP (PAGE 87)

Halve, seed, and dice the tomato. In a bowl, add the diced tomato, eggs, and oats, and whisk to combine. Add your choice of herbs or of spinach and feta. In a skillet, add a thin layer of oil, pour in the egg mixture, and cook over medium heat until the eggs are set. Season to taste with salt and pepper.
Slice the bagels or bread rolls in half, and spread each half with avocado dip. Divide the frittata between 2 bagel or bread roll bottoms, then top with remaining bread.

60

MORNING MUNCH

THE ULTIMATE SANDWICH

I simply adore sandwiches in the morning. You can use anything, whatever you have on hand, which often means yesterday's leftovers. Steak slices, strips of chicken, antipasti, boiled eggs from a picnic... the possibilities are endless. Raid your cooler bag and get creative!

4 SLICES OF WHOLEGRAIN BREAD
1 HEAPING TBSP QUARK,
SOUR CREAM, PESTO, OR HUMMUS
(PAGE 156)
1 RIPE AVOCADO
1 TOMATO, ½ ENGLISH CUCUMBER
2 HANDFULS OF ARUGULA
2 SLICES OF CHEESE SUCH AS GRUYÈRE
SALT AND BLACK PEPPER
FRESH SPROUTS
OR WATERCRESS

Spread each slice of bread with your choice of cheese, pesto, or hummus. Peel and pit the avocado. Slice the avocado, tomato, and cucumber, and cut the arugula leaves in half, if you wish.

To assemble the sandwiches, layer the ingredients onto two slices of bread, season to taste with salt and pepper, and add sprouts or watercress as desired. Top with the remaining 2 slices of bread.

SAVORY PANCAKES WITH COTTAGE CHEESE FILLING

A delicious and quick alternative to sweet pancakes, these pancakes are light and healthy, but still quite filling.

BATTER
1 CUP SPELT FLOUR
1 CUP MILK
2 EGGS
2 TBSP GRATED PARMESAN
PINCH EACH OF SALT AND BLACK PEPPER
FRESHLY CHOPPED MIXED HERBS
CANOLA OR SUNFLOWER OIL, FOR FRYING

FILLING
7 OZ (200 G) COTTAGE CHEESE
SALT AND BLACK PEPPER
1 TBSP PITTED OLIVES
1 DILL PICKLE
1 TOMATO
SPROUTS (OPTIONAL)

Make the filling: Season the cottage cheese to taste with salt and pepper. Halve the olives, and dice the pickle and the tomatoes. Fold them into the cottage cheese.

If you have sprouted some seeds, add a small handful or so of sprouts; they go really well with these pancakes. Make the batter: In a small bowl, whisk the flour and a bit of milk until smooth (to prevent lumps from forming later on). Whisk in the remaining milk, eggs, and Parmesan. Season with salt and pepper, and sprinkle in the herbs.

In a skillet, heat the oil over medium heat. Ladle 2 tablespoons of batter onto the skillet for each pancake. Cook on one side until golden brown, flip, and repeat. To serve, spoon some cottage cheese filling onto each pancake then fold or roll it up. Or, spread filling between 2 pancakes for a breakfast "sandwich."

BOULDERING

A CREATIVE AND FREE WAY OF MOVING

When the first boulderers walked
through local mountains and woods with
large, mattress-like crash pads strapped
to their backs, most hikers, Alpine
farmers and hut-keepers were astonished
to see these quirky, muscly people.

Bouldering has since become a hot sport.
Indoor climbing walls are sprouting up
everywhere, and new rock climbing areas
are being discovered and organized. There
has been an official Bouldering World
Championship for over 10 years.

But what exactly is bouldering, and how
did it start? Since the 1960s, bouldering
has been used more and more by climbers
for training purposes. It's a type of
climbing, but there is no rope and you
climb just far enough from the ground
that you can jump down safely. Below, for
safety, there are crash pads (portable
padded mattresses), and "spotters": other
boulderers who, in the event of a fall,
help guide the falling climber with
their outstretched arms onto the crash
pad. Bouldering is a young, standalone
sport, and a very social one at that. A
boulderer is seldom alone for long. When
trying to work out a boulder problem,
"better together" often applies.
The encouragement from other climbers
and the help of your spotter definitely
keeps you going!

QUICK ABCs OF BOULDERING

CHALK BAG: A bag filled with magnesium carbonate powder (aka chalk) to keep hands dry and improve grip.

CRASH PAD: A portable padded mattress.

DYNO: A dynamic leap to the next hold.

FB GRADES: The most widely used grading system for boulder problems in Europe. It was developed in Fontainebleau, near Paris.

FLASH: The successful completion of a boulder problem on the first try.

GROUNDER: A fall to the ground. Best avoid this!

HEEL HOOK: A climbing technique using the heel.

HIGHBALL: Taller than average boulders—falling off can be dangerous!

MANTLING: A climbing technique using your hands to push down rather than pull up.

PROBLEM: A defined bouldering route.

SPOTTING: Helping a falling climber safely onto the crash pad.

TOE HOOK: A climbing technique using the toe.

QUICK REFUEL

FAST POWER FOOD

Exploring nature, doing sports, just generally being active in the fresh outdoor air
will make you hungry and you know it. Are you heading back to the van for
a quick lunch? Then this section has got you covered, with delicious, healthy lunch
recipes that are fast to prepare and packed with energy for the second part
of your day. If you are planning on spending the whole day outdoors, some of these
recipes make perfect packable trail food. On day-long hikes you will be
grateful for good food. Picture yourself at the foot of the summit cross; why chew
on pieces of dry bread, or, worse even, tear open packets of energy gel when you can
pull out all the stops and celebrate the summit climb in epicurean style?
As we Bavarians say, "wer ko, der ko": Those who can do it, do it!

PANZANELLA

This salad uses up leftover bread perfectly.

½ BAGUETTE OR
2–3 DAY-OLD BREAD ROLLS
2 TBSP OLIVE OIL
1–2 GARLIC CLOVES
20 RIPE CHERRY TOMATOES
OR 4–5 RIPE VINE TOMATOES
1 LARGE RED ONION
2 HANDFULS BASIL LEAVES

DRESSING
2 TBSP RED OR WHITE WINE VINEGAR
4 TBSP OLIVE OIL
1 TSP BROWN SUGAR
SALT AND BLACK PEPPER

Make the salad: Cut the bread into cubes. In a skillet, heat the olive oil. Add the bread and sauté until golden brown. As soon as the bread starts to brown, press the garlic in a garlic press, add it to the skillet, and sauté briefly. Dice the tomatoes and the onion. Reserve a few basil leaves for garnish, and cut the rest into strips using kitchen shears. Transfer all salad ingredients into a bowl and toss to combine.

Make the dressing: Put all the ingredients in a screw-top jar and shake, or mix in a small bowl. Season to taste with salt and pepper.
Pour the dressing over the salad just before serving; don't let it sit too long. Serve garnished with the reserved basil leaves.

CAESAR SALAD

1–2 ROMAINE LETTUCES OR ROMAINE LETTUCE HEARTS, ½ BAGUETTE OR 1 DAY-OLD BUN,
2 TBSP OLIVE OIL. FOR THE DRESSING: 1 GARLIC CLOVE, 1 EGG YOLK, 1 TSP MUSTARD,
1 ORGANIC LEMON, 6 TBSP OLIVE OIL, ½ TSP RAW CANE SUGAR, SALT AND BLACK PEPPER, FRESHLY
SHAVED PARMESAN, AVOCADO OR STRIPS OF ROAST CHICKEN BREAST

Make the salad: Wash, spin, and coarsely chop the lettuce. Cut the bread into cubes. In a skillet heat 2 tablespoons of the olive oil, add the bread, and sauté until golden brown. Make the dressing: Finely chop the garlic. In a small bowl, whisk the egg yolk and the mustard; add the garlic. Wash the lemon in hot water and zest it, then juice it. Add both zest and juice to the egg yolk mixture. Add the remaining olive oil a few drops at a time, whisking constantly, until fully emulsified. Add the sugar and season with salt and pepper to taste.

Pour dressing over the salad and toss. Top with the croutons and generous shavings of Parmesan. For a light main course, serve with strips of roast chicken breast or avocado slices, as desired.

ORANGE AND FENNEL SALAD
WITH FETA CHEESE

This salad travels well (in a container with a tight-fitting lid!), and it comes together quickly as a side dish for fish or poultry. It also makes an excellent light snack, especially if garnished with toasted pine nuts or other nuts of your choice.

1 FENNEL BULB
1 KOHLRABI (OPTIONAL)
2 ORANGES
5 ½ OZ (150 G) FETA
FRESH HERBS,
SUCH AS BASIL OR
PARSLEY

DRESSING
2 TBSP WHITE BALSAMIC
OR FRUIT VINEGAR
3 TBSP OLIVE OIL
½ TSP TURMERIC (OPTIONAL)
½ TSP RAW CANE SUGAR
SALT AND BLACK PEPPER

Trim and core the fennel, reserving the fronds. Slice the fennel into thin strips. Trim and slice the kohlrabi, if using. Peel the oranges and remove the pith with a sharp paring knife. Cut the orange into pieces (save any juice and add it to the salad bowl). Dice or crumble the feta; chop the herbs and the fennel fronds. Transfer all salad ingredients into a salad bowl and toss.

Make the dressing: In a bowl, whisk together all ingredients. Pour the dressing over the salad, and let stand to absorb the flavors for 10 minutes before serving.

TABOULEH

Tabouleh works brilliantly as a take-along in a container with a tight-fitting lid, a quick side dish, or a nourishing snack.

2–3 CUPS ORGANIC VEGETABLE STOCK
½ TSP RAS EL HANOUT
(MOROCCAN SPICE MIX)
SALT AND BLACK PEPPER
1 CUP INSTANT COUSCOUS
OR BULGUR WHEAT
1–2 GARLIC CLOVES
2 LARGE RIPE TOMATOES
1 BELL PEPPER
1 CARROT
3 LEEKS OR 1 RED ONION
1 BUNCH FLAT-LEAF PARSLEY
1 ORGANIC LEMON
4 TBSP OLIVE OIL
FRESHLY CHOPPED MINT
OR CHILI FLAKES

Bring the stock to a boil and season with ras el hanout, salt and pepper. Put the couscous in a bowl, pour the stock over it, and let it stand until all liquid is absorbed. (Bulgur wheat will take longer to absorb the liquid, and may require more liquid plus boiling for a few minutes. Follow instructions on the package.)

Mince the garlic. Dice the tomatoes, pepper, carrot, and onions. Chop the parsley. When the couscous or bulgur wheat has cooled, transfer all ingredients into a large bowl and toss to combine.

Wash the lemon in hot water, zest it, and juice it. Add the lemon zest, lemon juice, and olive oil to the bowl. Adjust seasonings and let the tabouleh absorb some of the dressing. Garnish with mint or chili flakes, as desired, and serve.

QUINOA SALAD

Quinoa is THE power seed. A staple in the Inca Empire, it is gluten-free, rich in protein and omega-3 fatty acids, and ideal for those with active lifestyles! It also makes a tasty lunch on the road. Serve it alongside the refreshing yogurt-lemon dip (page 87).

½ CUP QUINOA
1–1 ½ CUPS ORGANIC VEGETABLE STOCK
½ WHITE OR RED ONION,
OR 1 SHALLOT
1 TOMATO
1 BELL PEPPER
½ BUNCH PARSLEY OR CILANTRO
4 TBSP FRESHLY SQUEEZED LEMON JUICE
OR WHITE BALSAMIC VINEGAR
4 TBSP EXTRA VIRGIN OLIVE OIL
SALT AND BLACK PEPPER,
TO TASTE
HOT SAUCE (SUCH AS SRIRACHA),
OLIVES, FETA CHEESE

Rinse and drain the quinoa. In a medium saucepan, add the quinoa and stock and bring to a boil. Reduce to a simmer and cook for 15 minutes. Remove from heat and let stand for 5 minutes, or until all liquid is absorbed.

Peel and dice the onion or shallot, the tomato, and the bell pepper. Add the vegetables to the quinoa immediately (or sauté them briefly with some olive oil, then add to the quinoa). Finely chop the parsley or cilantro and add to the salad.

Whisk together the lemon juice or vinegar and olive oil, and season to taste with salt and pepper. Add the dressing to the quinoa salad, adjust seasonings, and toss. Quinoa Salad also pairs well with grilled fish, meat, or falafel (page 84).

PERFECT TOMATO SALAD

For a truly perfect tomato salad you need perfectly ripe tomatoes.
Tomatoes should never see the inside of a refrigerator or a cooler bag
because they only reveal their full flavor at room temperature!

6 MEDIUM VINE TOMATOES
½ WHITE OR RED ONION,
OR 1 SHALLOT
½ BUNCH PARSLEY, CHIVES, OR BASIL
3 TBSP BALSAMIC VINEGAR
4 TBSP EXTRA VIRGIN OLIVE OIL
PINCH OF SUGAR
SALT AND BLACK PEPPER

Cut each tomato into 8 pieces. Peel and
finely dice the onion; chop the herbs.
Transfer the tomatoes and diced onion to a bowl.
Add the sugar, season to taste with salt and
pepper, and drizzle in the vinegar.
Toss to combine, then add the olive oil and
herbs. Let marinate for 5 minutes.

Adjust the seasonings and serve as a
side dish, or enjoy with crusty baguette
slices as a light lunch.

BRUSCHETTA AND CROSTINI

Crostini and bruschetta are classic Italian appetizers. They are colorful and versatile, and sure to please everyone at the table.

Crostini are usually served with a spread. Bruschetta are drizzled with olive oil and topped with tomatoes, for a classic bruschetta, or a variety of other toppings. Either way, the bread is toasted beforehand, and if you bring along some homemade pesto and other spreads, these savory toasts are a breeze to put together.

The secret to making these crispy delights is to start with a good baguette or ciabatta. Plain or whole grain, with olives or sun-dried tomatoes—use whatever tastes good to you. Grill or toast the bread just until golden brown on both sides; use a grill, the oven, or a skillet. Once toasted, let the bread cool.

CROSTINI

You can spread the crostini with tuna or avocado dip (page 87) or a pesto (page 27), then creatively top and garnish them with prosciutto, olives, and capers. Or, indulge your sweet tooth and top crostini with creamy goat cheese, fresh figs, walnuts, and a drizzle of honey.

BRUSCHETTA

2 RIPE TOMATOES OR
10 RIPE CHERRY TOMATOES
½ WHITE OR RED ONION
1 GARLIC CLOVE
10 BASIL LEAVES
2 TBSP OLIVE OIL
SALT AND BLACK PEPPER
4–6 SLICES BAGUETTE OR CIABATTA, TOASTED

Dice the tomatoes and onion; mince the garlic. Transfer to a bowl, add olive oil and basil leaves, season to taste with salt and pepper, and toss to combine. To serve, top each slice of toasted bread with some of the tomato mixture, drizzle with olive oil, and season to taste with more freshly ground black pepper.

TIP:
For a more summery, fruity bruschetta, add cubed melon and freshly chopped mint to the tomato mixture.

CUTTING AN ONION
HOW TO DO IT THE RIGHT WAY

Before the slicing and dicing comes the peeling. This is easily done with a
small paring knife. If the peel is hard to remove, or if you want to peel a lot of onions,
blanch the onions in hot water first. This makes the peel flexible and easier to
remove. Cut off the stem end (the top part) of the onion, but do not cut off the root end
(the "hairy" end of the onion with the tiny roots); this will hold the onion together
while you cut. Inspect the onion: if you see mold or soft brown spots, remove them or even
throw out the whole thing. Mold spreads in onions without always being visible,
but it is a health risk—not to mention it tastes musty.

Now, cut the onion in half lengthwise—from root end to stem—with a sharp knife.
(Using a dull knife will release the essential oils, which is why onions make you cry.)

Place the onion halves on a cutting board cut-side down. Now get ready for showtime!
There are several different cuts to learn, but most recipes call for onions to be finely diced
(brunoise) or thinly sliced (julienne), as, for example, in tomato salads or ceviche.

The safest way to hold an onion is to use the "claw hold": curl the fingertips of the hand
holding the onion slightly inwards, like a claw, and use your knuckles to guide the knife.

To finely dice an onion: Make several vertical, evenly spaced cuts from the root end of the
onion to the tip. Then, holding the onion steady, make horizontal slices towards the root end,
spaced the same as your vertical cuts. This determines the size of your dice.
Now, make evenly spaced vertical cuts perpendicular to your first ones. Discard the root.

To thinly slice an onion: Simply make evenly spaced vertical cuts into the onion half.
If you want to make onion rings, do not cut the onion in half,
and always start cutting at the tip of the onion.

FALAFEL

14 OZ (400 G) CANNED CHICKPEAS, DRAINED, OR 1 CUP CHICKPEA FLOUR MIXED WITH BROTH
1 RED OR WHITE ONION
2 GARLIC CLOVES
1 SMALL BUNCH PARSLEY OR CILANTRO
1 EGG YOLK
1 TBSP BREADCRUMBS OR 1 TSP BAKING POWDER
2 TBSP ALL-PURPOSE FLOUR
½ TSP GROUND CUMIN
½ TSP HUNGARIAN PAPRIKA
SALT AND BLACK PEPPER
CANOLA, SUNFLOWER, OR PEANUT OIL, FOR FRYING

In a bowl, puree the well-drained chickpeas using a fork (or an immersion blender, if available). Finely chop the onion, garlic, and herbs, and add them to the chickpea puree. Add the remaining ingredients and mix to make a sturdy dough. Moisten your hands with water and shape dough into small balls. In a deep frying pan, heat about 2 inches of oil, but don't let it smoke. Fry the balls in batches until golden brown. (The oil will be hot, so keep children away!) Using a slotted spoon, remove the falafel and drain on paper towels.

Falafel pairs especially well with dips such as hummus or yogurt-lemon (pages 86-87), which you can tweak by adding freshly chopped mint, as well as slices of English cucumber. Traditionally, falafel is eaten stuffed inside pita pockets or served with flatbread on the side, but it also makes a good addition to salads, picnics, and other cold collations, just like meatballs.

TIP:

If you don't have enough oil with you to cover the falafel when frying, shape the chickpea puree into flat patties instead.

HuMMUS

14 OZ (400 G) CANNED COOKED CHICKPEAS, RINSED AND DRAINED,
JUICE OF 1 LEMON, ½ GARLIC CLOVE, MINCED, 1 TBSP OLIVE OIL, 1–2 TBSP TAHINI
(SESAME PASTE), GROUND CUMIN, SALT AND BLACK PEPPER, PARSLEY AND
CILANTRO LEAVES, CHOPPED

In a bowl, mash the chickpeas using a fork. Add the lemon juice, garlic,
olive oil, and tahini, and mix well until creamy. Season to taste with cumin,
salt and pepper. Garnish with parsley or coriander leaves.

DIPS

Served with raw vegetables cut into sticks,
these dips make a perfect snack on the trail.

YOGURT-LEMON DIP

1 CUP PLAIN GREEK YOGURT, JUICE OF ½ LEMON,
CHOPPED FRESH HERBS (SUCH AS BASIL, PARSLEY, OR CILANTRO,
IF AVAILABLE), SALT AND BLACK PEPPER

In a bowl, add the yogurt, lemon juice, and your herbs of choice,
and mix to combine. Season to taste with salt and pepper.
To turn the dip into an excellent salad dressing, add a pinch of
sugar, a minced garlic clove, and 1 tablespoon olive oil.

TUNA DIP

6 OZ (170 G) CANNED TUNA, IN ITS JUICES, OR SALMON, OR
MACKEREL, JUICE OF ½ LEMON, HANDFUL OF CHIVES OR PARSLEY,
CHOPPED, ½ RED ONION, DICED, SALT AND BLACK PEPPER

In a bowl, mash the tuna or other fish. Add the
lemon juice, herbs, and onion, and mix to make a creamy dip.
Season to taste with salt and pepper.

AVOCADO DIP

1 RIPE AVOCADO, JUICE OF ½ LEMON, HOT SAUCE (SUCH AS
SRIRACHA), SALT AND BLACK PEPPER, ½ GARLIC CLOVE, MINCED,
½ TOMATO, FINELY DICED, FRESH HERBS OF CHOICE (OPTIONAL)

Peel and pit the avocado. In a bowl, add the
avocado and lemon juice, and mash with a fork.
Add the garlic, tomato, and herbs, if using.
Season to taste with hot sauce, salt and pepper.

OUTDOOR EATING AT ITS BEST

A picnic—a "brotzeit" as we say in Germany—tastes good anytime, anywhere. A colorful picnic blanket can become a canvas for delicious nibbles in no time, as long as you've packed some basics. Here are some tips and tricks for whipping up the perfect *brotzeit*.

SUMMIT PICNIC

Backpacks are always packed to optimize space and weight. Some things are not optional (you must always carry enough water!), but you can also make room for small pleasures. Personally, I often enjoy a celebratory beer at the summit, or an espresso courtesy of my small moka pot. Everything I have on hand is portable. In my picnic box you will usually find bread; smoked bacon; sausage; cheese; tomatoes; and dill pickles; bananas, for quick and lasting energy; apples, to cleanse and refresh. Cook a few extra eggs at breakfast, or wrap up yesterday's leftovers and bring them along. Fresh cheeses (ricotta, sour cream, goat cheese) are also good for bringing along: they don't melt as quickly as butter, and they work equally well as bread toppings as they do for dipping veggie sticks.

LUXURY PICNIC

For a sophisticated spin on any picnic, a cooler bag is a must. This allows you to serve delicacies at the right temperature.
A bottle of Prosecco, some smoked salmon, paper-thin slices of ham—everything tastes better when it is properly chilled.
And don't forget plates, silverware, and glasses: bring very light bamboo plates, plastic wine glasses that piece together, a small cutting board, kitchen towel, some napkins, and a few tealights.

If you are bringing wine, don't forget the corkscrew! But if you do, try this: cut the foil with a knife, wrap a towel around the bottom of the bottle, and lightly tap the side of the bottle against a tree. Bit by bit, the cork will be expelled until it can finally be pulled out easily. The recipes in this book complement each other. The many mouth-watering dips, salads, sandwiches, and wraps will elevate your picnic basket to a portable tapas bar. Your picnic will be the highlight of the day!

DON'T LEAVE HOME WITHOUT THESE:

For starters, a sharp knife; it will make short work of cutting up salami, smoked bacon, cheese, dill pickles, or tomatoes. For safety, choose one that folds or has a sheath.

Salt and black peppercorns. There are countless small salt and pepper mills and waterproof shakers available—you won't regret bringing one along.

A picnic blanket, or foldable insulating cushions. Depending on how far you are going and how much room there is in your backpack, these may not be a necessity; they will, however, keep you dry and much more comfortable when sitting on the ground.

FUNKY TUNA SANDWICH

Sandwiches make fantastic traveling companions. Whether relaxing on the beach, enjoying a hike, or just sitting outside the van, when you pull out this funky tuna sandwich... prepare to share!

1 PLAIN OR OLIVE CIABATTA LOAF
1 TBSP OLIVE OIL
YOGURT-LEMON DIP (PAGE 87)
12 OZ (340 G) CANNED TUNA
2 TBSP SUN-DRIED TOMATOES, CHOPPED
½ BUNCH BASIL, LEAVES COARSELY CHOPPED
2 TBSP PITTED OLIVES, CHOPPED
1 AVOCADO
1 SMALL ENGLISH CUCUMBER
2 HARDBOILED EGGS
½ WHITE OR RED ONION, OR 1 SHALLOT
HANDFUL OF ARUGULA
SALT AND BLACK PEPPER

Cut the ciabatta in half lengthwise. If you wish, you can lightly toast the bread cut-side down, or brush the cut sides with olive oil and brown in a skillet. Spread each half with yogurt-lemon dip.

Drain the tuna. In a bowl, add the tuna, sun-dried tomatoes, basil, and olives, and mix to combine. Season to taste with salt and pepper.

On the bottom half of the ciabatta, spread the tuna mixture. Slice the avocado, cucumber, eggs, and onion or shallot, and layer over the tuna. Scatter arugula leaves and a generous sprinkling of pepper on top.

Top sandwich with the remaining ciabatta half and press down lightly. Cut the sandwich in half, and wrap it tightly in waxed paper if you are taking it with you.

CLUB TORTILLA WRAP

A rolled-up tortilla can accommodate a lot, not least yesterday's leftovers (think thinly-sliced steak, couscous, quinoa, or grilled vegetables). Mix-and-match your ingredients of choice, and add a sauce or dip for extra succulence.

1 SMALL ROMAINE LETTUCE
1–2 TOMATOES
1 SKINLESS, BONELESS
CHICKEN BREAST
1 TBSP OLIVE OIL
4 SLICES BACON
2 LARGE TORTILLAS
AVOCADO DIP AND
YOGURT-LEMON DIP (PAGE 87)
BARBECUE SEASONING
OR HUNGARIAN PAPRIKA
SALT AND BLACK PEPPER

Cut the lettuce into wide strips; dice the tomatoes. Rub the chicken with salt, barbecue seasoning or paprika, and pepper. In a pan, heat the olive oil over medium heat, and cook the chicken until golden brown on all sides.
Add the bacon to the pan and fry until crisp. Remove both meats from the pan, reserving the oil and bacon drippings. Slice the chicken breast.

In the same pan, heat the tortillas on both sides. To assemble, lay the tortillas out flat and spread each with avocado dip. Divide the lettuce, tomatoes, chicken, and bacon evenly between the tortillas, leaving about a third free at the top. Drizzle with yogurt-lemon dip and season with pepper. Fold the sides of each tortilla slightly inwards. Pressing lightly, roll up each tortilla from bottom to top.

TIP:

Roll the tortillas up more tightly and firmly, then pack them in plastic wrap.
Just before serving, cut the tortilla wraps slightly on the diagonal into inch-thick pieces.
The result? Fabulous bite-sized tapas with great visual appeal.
After all, no matter how food is served—on a small cutting board, picnic blanket,
or festive buffet—first, you feast with the eyes.

QUICK SPAGHETTI CARBONARA WITH AVOCADO

This vegetarian spin on carbonara is quick, healthy, and always a big hit!

9 OZ (250 G) WHOLE GRAIN SPAGHETTI, SUCH AS LIGHT SPELT OR KAMUT
AVOCADO DIP WITH GARLIC AND TOMATO (PAGE 87)
GRATED PARMESAN, CHOPPED PARSLEY

Fill a large pot with salted water and bring to a boil. Add the pasta and cook until al dente. Drain the pasta, reserving a cup of the pasta cooking water. In the same pot, mix some avocado dip with pasta water until it reaches your desired consistency, and season to taste with salt, pepper, Parmesan, and parsley. Return spaghetti to the pot, toss with the sauce, adjust the seasonings, and serve.

SUPER FAST SPAGHETTI CARBONARA

½ BUNCH PARSLEY
7 OZ (200 G) HEAVY CREAM
2 EGG YOLKS
4 TBSP GRATED PARMESAN
9 OZ (250 G) WHOLE GRAIN SPAGHETTI, SUCH AS LIGHT SPELT OR KAMUT
½ ONION
1 GARLIC CLOVE
5 ½ OZ (150 G) SMOKED BACON
1 TBSP OLIVE OIL OR UNSALTED BUTTER
SALT AND BLACK PEPPER
½ RED CHILI PEPPER (OPTIONAL)

Pick the parsley leaves from the stems and finely chop. Dice the onion, crush the garlic, and cube or thinly slice the bacon. In a bowl, add the parsley, cream, egg yolks, and Parmesan, and lightly whisk to combine. Season generously with salt and pepper.

Fill a large pot with salted water and bring to a boil. Add the pasta and cook until al dente. Drain the pasta, reserving a cup of the cooking water. In the same pot, heat the olive oil or butter. Add the onion, garlic, bacon, and chili, if using. Cook until the onion is soft and translucent. Return spaghetti to the pot, and toss well to combine. If it sticks together, add some of the pasta water.

Reduce heat to the lowest setting, and pour the egg mixture into the pot. Mixing constantly, cook until the sauce has barely thickened but do not let it curdle, so work quickly and remove from heat promptly. Serve immediately.

QUICK SPAGHETTI
CARBONARA WITH AVOCADO

SUPER FAST SPAGHETTI
CARBONARA

QUESADILLAS

GREEK QUESADILLA

HANDFUL OF BABY SPINACH LEAVES
2 TBSP OIL-PACKED SUN-DRIED
TOMATOES, DRAINED
2 TBSP PITTED OLIVES, IDEALLY KALAMATA
3 ½ OZ (100 G) FETA CHEESE
3 ½ OZ (100 G) MOZZARELLA CHEESE, IDEALLY
FRESH (BUFFALO)
4 WHEAT OR CORN TORTILLAS
SALT AND BLACK PEPPER

Coarsely chop the tomatoes, olives, feta, and mozzarella. Divide all ingredients between 2 tortillas and season with salt and pepper. Top with the remaining tortillas.

Heat a large skillet over medium heat. Add the quesadillas and cook until they are golden brown on both sides and the cheese has melted. (If your skillet is not large enough, cut the tortillas into quarters before filling them, or purchase slightly smaller tortillas.)

GOAT CHEESE QUESADILLA

4 TBSP WALNUTS
1 PEACH
2 SLICES GOAT CHEESE,
PREFERABLY FROM A LOG
2 TSP HONEY
1 SPRIG FRESH ROSEMARY
HANDFUL OF ARUGULA
4 WHEAT OR CORN TORTILLAS
SALT AND BLACK PEPPER

Coarsely chop the walnuts. Slice the peach. Divide the walnuts, peach slices, goat cheese, honey, and arugula between 2 tortillas. Sprinkle with rosemary and season with salt and pepper. Top with the remaining tortillas.

Heat a large skillet over medium heat. Add the quesadillas and cook until they are golden brown on both sides and the cheese has melted. (If your skillet is not large enough, cut the tortillas into quarters before filling them, or purchase slightly smaller tortillas.)

TORTILLA ESPAÑOLA

Not to be confused with the flatbread-style tortillas used for quesadillas and burritos, a tortilla española is a classic Spanish omelet with onions and potatoes. It is equally scrumptious served hot or cold, and one of the best-suited snacks for the trail or the road.

6 MEDIUM YUKON GOLD POTATOES
4 TBSP OLIVE OIL
1 WHITE OR RED ONION
3-4 EGGS
½ BUNCH PARSLEY OR CHIVES
HANDFUL OF BELL PEPPERS,
GREEN ASPARAGUS,
OR MUSHROOMS (OPTIONAL)
SALT AND BLACK PEPPER
CHILI POWDER

Peel and thinly slice the potatoes.
Dice the onion. If using, chop the bell peppers, asparagus, or mushrooms. In a skillet, heat the olive oil over medium heat. Add the potato slices and sauté until almost cooked through but not starting to brown. Add the onion and chopped vegetables, if using, and sauté briefly with the potatoes. Season generously with salt and pepper.

In a bowl, break the eggs. Finely chop the parsley or chives, add to the eggs, and whisk together. Flatten the potatoes with a spatula and pour the egg mixture evenly over the potatoes.

Reduce heat to low. Without stirring, cook the potato and egg mixture until the eggs are completely set. Then, set a large plate over the tortilla, hold it down with one hand, and flip the skillet upside down with the other. Slide the tortilla from the plate back into the skillet, and continue to cook until done.

TYROLEAN FARMERS' HASH

Best served straight from a cast-iron skillet so people can help
themselves, Tyrolean Hash is accompanied by thick slices of sourdough
bread and unsalted butter. Take a bite, close your eyes,
and picture yourself in a cabin in the Alps...

4–6 MEDIUM COOKED POTATOES
2 TBSP OLIVE OIL
4 SLICES SMOKED BACON
1 WHITE OR RED ONION
½ TBSP UNSALTED BUTTER
½ TSP CARAWAY SEEDS
2–4 EGGS
½ BUNCH PARSLEY
OR CHIVES
½ TSP DRIED OREGANO
SALT AND BLACK PEPPER

Peel and slice the potatoes, cut the bacon into
strips, and slice the onions. In a cast-iron
skillet or frying pan, heat the olive oil.
Add the potatoes and cook until golden brown.
Add the bacon, onions, butter, and caraway
seeds, and sauté until they start to color.

In a bowl, whisk the eggs and pour evenly over
the potato hash. Season liberally with pepper
and sprinkle with the herbs, but go easy on the
salt (the bacon is salty enough). Cook until
eggs are set. Alternatively, you can fry up your
eggs separately.

TIP
Tyrolean Hash is particularly good for using leftovers such as
slices of steak or raw vegetables. For a great vegetarian variation, omit the bacon
and add blanched green beans cut in half. Using precooked potatoes ensures
you will have food on the table in no time.

HIKING

RELAXING OUTDOOR MEDITATION

"The path is the goal" is often quoted when talking about hiking. Hiking starts with
the most natural of human acts: walking in the mountains. It is the most widely
practiced form of contemplative movement, it satisfies our longing to commune with
nature directly, and it is an excellent way to rid ourselves of stress. Hiking
will never go out of style; in fact, its "renaissance" over the past several years is
proof of its versatility. You can hike almost anywhere; there is relatively little
need for equipment; hiking leaves a small environmental footprint (assuming you follow
some basic rules); and it is for people of all levels of ability and fitness. If you
are fit, you can crank up the difficulty. With specialized knowledge about altitude
and with the proper equipment, you can turn your hiking trips into mountain climbing
or rock climbing adventures, or even hike up over the snow into alpine terrain.
If increased speed and general conditioning are your goals, and you have the fitness
level for it, try trail running (jogging over hiking trails at a steady pace).
Hiking truly is for everyone: Where there's a will, there's a way.

WELL-EQUIPPED ON THE TRAIL

The hiking route is picked, the weather is good, your backpack is packed... but is
it packed well? Sure, you've got clothing, enough to drink, a first-aid kid, your
pocketknife. What about your salt and pepper mills? For most people, food is an
afterthought when it comes to packing for a hiking trip. I say it's time to change that.
The food you take on a trip is very important as a source of both energy and enjoyment.
In this book, the 🎒 icon denotes recipes that make good trail food. Here are some
things that I always take with me on the trail, because they are healthy, full of
long-lasting energy, small and lightweight, and also taste amazing: fresh fruits, like
apples and bananas, if available (bananas, in particular, give ample energy and plenty
of mineral nutrients); dried fruits and nuts; the trail mixes, bars, and squash cookies
in this book (pages 36-39), especially for multi-day trips and as emergency backups,
or for a quick burst of power. So next time you are puzzling over what to pack, go for
simple-but-good: bread, cheese, salami, hardboiled eggs, tomatoes, pickles. If you, like
me, want to have a summit (or trail's-end) picnic, make room for a picnic blanket, and
maybe add to the above yesterday's leftovers, or some small sandwiches and wraps. If
this sounds like a luxury, I argue that it isn't. The right food guarantees that you
will have more fun on your hike. Life is all about the small things!

DINING IN

COOKING ON ONE OR TWO
BURNERS IN THE VAN

Weather acting up? Rain gently pattering the roof? Are you and your van stranded
in the middle of a city or waiting out a snowstorm somewhere? Don't despair,
for there is a silver lining: you get to cocoon inside the van, in its heart and soul,
with some good music and a nice meal. This chapter will give you
recipe ideas for those days and nights spent inside your camper van. The recipes are
easy to cook in the van, and there's not much frying or sputtering of oil
involved; just beautiful aromas that will linger, but not stifle your snug space.
(At least for a couple of rainy days in a row; then the sunshine had better return!)

MOROCCAN SALAD with TOMATOES and CUCUMBER

I came to love this simple salad during my trips to Morocco.
The magic touch in this recipe is the use of fresh thyme.
A glorious snack on its own or with flatbread, it also makes a
refreshingly light side dish for fish, steak, or lamb.

4–6 VINE TOMATOES
1 ENGLISH CUCUMBER
½ MEDIUM RED OR WHITE ONION,
OR 1 SHALLOT
ZEST AND JUICE OF
AN ORGANIC LEMON,
OR 3–4 TBSP WHITE VINEGAR
3–4 SPRIGS OF FRESH THYME, PARSLEY,
OR CILANTRO
4 TBSP OLIVE OIL
SALT AND BLACK PEPPER

Seed the tomatoes and cut them into quarters.
Peel the cucumber and cut it in half lengthwise;
using a small spoon, scrape out the seeds,
then cut the cucumber halves into pieces about
the same size as the tomato quarters.

Finely chop the onion, zest then juice the
lemon, and pick the thyme leaves from the
sprigs. Transfer all ingredients to a
bowl, season to taste with salt and pepper,
and toss well.

PENNE WITH TUNA AND OLIVES

Another very easy dish made with ingredients you should
have on hand. Contrary to Italian pasta etiquette, which dictates that
you never add cheese to pasta containing fish or seafood, I actually
like Parmesan in this dish.

½ PACKAGE WHOLE GRAIN PENNE,
SUCH AS LIGHT SPELT
½ MEDIUM RED OR WHITE ONION,
OR 1 SHALLOT
1–2 GARLIC CLOVES
4 TBSP OLIVE OIL
6 OZ (170 G) CANNED TUNA
6 TBSP PITTED OLIVES
DRIED OREGANO
SALT AND BLACK PEPPER
CHILI FLAKES
14 OZ (400 G) CHOPPED CANNED TOMATOES
½ BUNCH PARSLEY AND
FRESHLY SHAVED PARMESAN

Fill a large pot with salted water and bring to
a boil. Add the pasta and cook until al dente.

While the pasta cooks, make the sauce. In a
saucepan, heat the oil. Finely chop the onion
and garlic, and add to the saucepan; cook
until soft and translucent. Add the tuna and
tomatoes, and season to taste with oregano,
salt, pepper, and chili flakes. Cut the olives
in half and add to the sauce.

Drain the pasta, return it to the pot, and pour
in the sauce. Toss well, sprinkle with freshly
chopped parsley and shaved Parmesan, and serve.

Spaghetti Bolognese

This sauce explodes with flavor, which only gets better the next day, and it keeps really well, too. Prepare the bolognese at home, freeze it in small portions, and take at least a few of them along. Then defrost it, cook some spaghetti, and voilà!

Ingredients	Instructions
1 SMALL CARROT	Trim and dice the carrot, celery, and onion; mince the garlic. In a large pan, heat the olive oil over medium heat. Add the onion and garlic, and sauté until soft and translucent. Add the ground beef and cook, breaking up any large pieces, until browned all over. Season generously with salt and pepper. When the meat is well-browned, deglaze with the wine. Add the tomatoes, oregano, and sugar, along with the diced vegetables. Simmer over medium heat until the vegetables are tender. Remove the stems from the parsley, rosemary, and thyme, finely chop the leaves, and add them to the sauce. Adjust the seasonings and add chili flakes, if desired. If the sauce is too thick, add some vegetable stock. In a large pot, add salted water and bring to a boil. Add the pasta and cook until al dente. Drain the pasta and return it to the pot. Add the bolognese sauce and toss well. Serve with shaved Parmesan on the side.
1 STALK CELERY	
1 RED OR WHITE ONION	
1–2 GARLIC CLOVES	
2 TBSP OLIVE OIL	
10 OZ (300 G) FRESH GROUND BEEF	
½ CUP (100 ML) RED WINE	
14 OZ (400 G) CHOPPED CANNED TOMATOES	
1 TSP DRIED OREGANO	
1 TSP SUGAR	
½ BUNCH PARSLEY	
1 SPRIG ROSEMARY	
1 SPRIG THYME	
9 OZ (250 G) LIGHT SPELT SPAGHETTI	
SALT AND BLACK PEPPER	
CHILI FLAKES	
FRESHLY GRATED PARMESAN	
½ CUP ORGANIC VEGETABLE STOCK, AS NEEDED	

TIP:

Make sure not to overcook the pasta. If it sticks together, reserve 1 cup of cooking water when draining the pasta. Return pasta to the pot and immediately add the cooking water. Stir once. (Don't use oil. This would prevent the pasta from absorbing the sauce, i. e. all the flavor!)

For a VEGETARIAN version: Crumble enough tofu to fill 1–2 cups.
Heat some organic vegetable stock. In a bowl, combine tofu and stock, and let soften.
Proceed as in recipe, substituting tofu for beef and adding 2 teaspoons of soy sauce for extra umami.

CEVICHE

Ceviche is South America's answer to sushi. It is said to
have originated in Lima, Peru. The first time I tried it was at a restaurant
famous for its ceviche, and it was a revelation—simple, refreshing,
and absolutely star-worthy.

For ceviche, using the freshest fish you can find is of the utmost
importance. Use the very best ingredients, but also know that there is
endless room for creativity. Experiment with different kinds of fish
until you find your favorite; fresh or saltwater fish will both do.
I am lucky enough to live in front of a lake, and always prefer to catch
my own perch or trout for ceviche. Enjoy experimenting!

---

10 OZ (300 G) FRESH BONELESS,
SKINLESS FISH FILLET
JUICE OF 2 LIMES OR 1 LEMON
SALT AND BLACK PEPPER
½ BUNCH CILANTRO OR PARSLEY
1 SMALL RED ONION
2 TBSP OLIVE OIL
½ RED CHILI PEPPER
1 SMALL PIECE FRESH GINGER
½ GARLIC CLOVE

Cut the fish fillet into small thin strips and
add to a bowl. Add the citrus juice and
mix gently to combine. Season to taste with salt
and pepper. The longer you marinate the fish
the more its proteins break down; this
"cooks" the fish. In my opinion, 10 minutes
is plenty of time.

Chop the cilantro or parsley and add it to
a small bowl. Slice the onion into very thin
rings and add to the herbs, along with the olive
oil; stir to combine. Finely dice the chili,
mince the ginger and the garlic, and add to
the bowl. Toss the fish with the herb dressing,
garnish with additional slices of onions and
herbs, and serve immediately.

TIP:

You can also use fresh mango, avocado, cucumber, corn, or leek in your own personalized ceviche.
The only rules to follow are that the ingredients be available, fresh, and taste good.

119

WHITE BEAN STEW WITH ITALIAN SAUSAGE

½ ONION OR 1 SHALLOT
1–2 GARLIC CLOVES
2–3 MILD ITALIAN SAUSAGES
2 TBSP OLIVE OR CANOLA OIL
1 SPRIG ROSEMARY
14 OZ (400 G) CANNED WHITE BEANS,
SUCH AS CANELLINI
14 OZ (400 G) CANNED CHOPPED TOMATOES
1 CUP ORGANIC VEGETABLE STOCK
2 STALKS CELERY
½ BUNCH PARSLEY
SALT AND BLACK PEPPER

Chop the onion, crush the garlic, and cut the sausages into small pieces. In a pot, heat the oil over medium heat. Add the sausage and cook until browned. Add the onion, garlic, and rosemary, and sauté until the onion is soft and translucent.

Drain the beans, add to the pot, and stir. Add the stock and tomatoes to the pot and deglaze. Cut the celery into ½ in (1 cm) pieces and add to the pot. Simmer until the celery is softened, about 10 minutes. Season to taste with salt and pepper, ladle into bowls, garnish with parsley, and serve.

VARIATIONS:

VEGETARIAN:
You can substitute carrots, or another root vegetable, for the sausage.

SPICY:
Substitute spicy chorizo or bratwurst sausages for the Italian sausage. Or, add finely diced chili pepper to the pot together with the onion and garlic, then add the zest of an organic lemon together with the beans.

Hearty Lentil Stew with Bacon and Potatoes

2 CARROTS	Scrub the potatoes and cut into ½ in (1 cm) cubes. Dice the onion, crush the garlic, and cube the bacon. Chop the carrots and dice the celery root or celery stalks. In a pot, heat the oil over medium heat. Add the bacon and cook until lightly browned. Add the onion and garlic and cook until soft and translucent.
¼ CELERY ROOT OR	
2 STALKS CELERY	
2–3 WAXY POTATOES, SUCH AS YUKON GOLD	
½ ONION OR 1 SHALLOT	
1 GARLIC CLOVE	
2 THICK SLICES SMOKED PORK BELLY BACON	Add the lentils to the pot and stir, then add the vinegar and deglaze the pot by scraping up the tasty bits from the bottom. Add the carrots, celery root or celery, and potatoes. Pour in the stock, bring to a boil, then reduce heat to medium and simmer until the lentils and potatoes are cooked, about 15 minutes. Season to taste with salt and pepper, and garnish with chopped parsley leaves.
2 TBSP OLIVE OIL OR CANOLA OIL	
½ CUP RED OR YELLOW LENTILS, PICKED THROUGH AND RINSED	
4 TBSP BALSAMIC VINEGAR	
3–4 CUPS ORGANIC VEGETABLE STOCK	
½ BUNCH PARSLEY	
SALT AND BLACK PEPPER	

VARIATIONS:

VEGETARIAN:
Simply omit the bacon; the stew is just as hearty without it.

HEARTIER:
Add pieces of sausage to the pot together with the bacon.
Try kielbasa, debrecener (or debreziner), or any other smoked pork sausage of choice.

PORTUGUESE FISH STEW

2 RED OR YELLOW BELL PEPPERS
2 ONIONS
6 YUKON GOLD OR RUSSET POTATOES
10 OZ (300 G) FIRM-FLESHED FISH FILLET, SUCH AS MONKFISH OR PIKE
2 GARLIC CLOVES
1 MILD CHILI PEPPER
14 OZ (400 G) CHOPPED CANNED TOMATOES
½ CUP (100 ML) WHITE WINE
½ CUP (100 ML) WATER
4 TBSP OLIVE OIL
GROUND SAFFRON OR TURMERIC
HUNGARIAN PAPRIKA
SALT AND BLACK PEPPER
CAYENNE PEPPER
1 BUNCH CILANTRO

Slice the bell peppers and onions; thinly slice the garlic and chili pepper; peel the potatoes and cut into ½ in (1 cm) thick slices. Cut the fish into bite-sized pieces.

In a large pot, layer the ingredients in the following order: onions, bell peppers, chili pepper and garlic, potatoes, tomatoes, and fish, ending with a top layer of vegetables. Sprinkle each layer liberally with the saffron or turmeric, paprika, salt, and both kinds of peppers.

When all ingredients are layered, pour the wine and water into the pot, and drizzle in the olive oil. Top the final layer with half of the cilantro. Cover the pot, bring to a boil, reduce heat to low, and simmer for about 15 minutes. Remove from heat and let rest for 10 minutes.

Chop the leaves from the remaining half bunch of cilantro. Ladle the stew into bowls, garnish with cilantro, and serve with thick baguette slices and chilled white wine. Unless you have a refrigerator, the stew is best on the day it is made.

TIP:

If you don't like cilantro, you can use parsley instead; both taste good.
Also, feel free to swap out one vegetable for another. Freshwater and saltwater fish both work in this recipe; use what you will, as long as the fish has a firm flesh that will hold together.
To jazz up the recipe, add mussels or prawns.

~Thai Curry with Rice

This curry takes me back to the many evenings I cooked it for friends, and friends of friends, in Australian hostels. With everyone helping to cut up the veggies, prep time is reduced and the recipe can be scaled up to feed a crowd. The order in which you add the vegetables is important. They have different cooking times; I always add the softer ones at the end so that they retain some bite.

1 LB 2 OZ (500 G) ASSORTED VEGETABLES
1 SKINLESS, BONELESS CHICKEN BREAST
1 TBSP SOY SAUCE
1 TSP HONEY
1 ONION, 1–2 GARLIC CLOVES
2 TBSP CANOLA OIL
2–3 TBSP THAI CURRY PASTE
⅔ CUP (150 ML) COCONUT MILK
1 CUP BASMATI OR JASMINE RICE
1½ CUPS WATER
SALT AND BLACK PEPPER
FRESHLY GRATED GINGER (OPTIONAL)
1 RED CHILI PEPPER (OPTIONAL)
FRESHLY CHOPPED PARSLEY
OR CILANTRO

Cut the chicken into pieces and transfer to a small bowl. Whisk together the soy sauce and honey, and add to the bowl. Season with salt and pepper, and turn chicken pieces to coat. Cover with plastic wrap and marinate in the refrigerator for at least 1 hour. Cut the vegetables into large, uniform pieces. Set aside, keeping each vegetable separate, since they will be added into the wok or pan in a different order. Finely chop the onion and garlic. In a wok or a large pan or skillet, heat the canola oil. Add the garlic and onions, and briefly sauté; add the curry paste and the chili and ginger, if using, and stir. Add the chicken, brown it briefly, then add the coconut milk. Add your choice of vegetables starting with the harder ones, such as carrots, and adding spinach or sprouts last. Check and adjust the seasonings, and simmer over low heat until the chicken is cooked through and the vegetables have reached the desired doneness. Meanwhile, in a separate pot, cook the rice according to the package instructions.

Garnish the curry with cilantro or parsley, and serve over or alongside the fragrant rice.

TIP:

There is a lot of flexibility with the vegetables; use whatever is in season and/or available. Typically, carrots, sugar snap peas, bok choy, and fresh spinach all work well. For a smoother texture, try squash, potatoes, or eggplant.

CHICKPEA CURRY

1 ONION, 2 GARLIC CLOVES
2 TBSP CANOLA OIL
THUMB OF FRESH GINGER
(ABOUT 1 INCH LONG)
1 SMALL RED CHILI PEPPER
3–4 RIPE BEEFSTEAK TOMATOES
OR 14 OZ (400 G) CHOPPED CANNED TOMATOES
14 OZ (400 G) CANNED CHICKPEAS,
RINSED AND DRAINED
½ TSP BROWN SUGAR
½ TSP EACH GROUND CORIANDER, CUMIN,
TURMERIC, AND GARAM MASALA,
OR 1 TBSP RAS EL HANOUT
SALT AND BLACK PEPPER
½ BUNCH PARSLEY, CILANTRO,
OR BABY SPINACH
STRIPS OF FRIED CHICKEN BREAST
(OPTIONAL)

Roughly chop the onion and garlic; finely dice the ginger; seed and chop the chili; finely chop the tomatoes. In a pot or deep frying pan, heat the oil. Add the onion and garlic, and sauté briefly; add the ginger and chili pepper to the pot and give it a few stirs; add the sugar and spices, and season to taste with salt and pepper.

Add tomatoes to the pot. Lower the heat to a simmer, and cook for 10 minutes. Add the drained chickpeas to the tomato mixture and bring to a boil. Remove from heat and check and adjust the seasonings. Garnish with fresh parsley, cilantro, or baby spinach leaves. Top with strips of fried chicken breast, if using. Serve with Indian naan or another flatbread, or with rice.

TIP:

Leftover chickpea curry also tastes great cold, tucked inside flatbread, when you are on the road.

MaNGO SaLaD

This unusual salad is best eaten warm,
and it tastes spectacular served with grilled fish.

1 CUP WILD RICE
1 MANGO
½ CUP FROZEN PEAS
1 HANDFUL EACH CHOPPED LEEKS
AND INCH-LONG PIECES OF ASPARAGUS
(OPTIONAL)
FRESH MIXED HERBS,
SUCH AS CILANTRO, BASIL, OR MINT
1 ORGANIC LEMON
2 TBSP OLIVE OIL
1 TSP MAPLE SYRUP, HONEY,
OR BROWN SUGAR
SALT AND BLACK PEPPER

Wash the rice thoroughly. In a pot, bring 4 cups of unsalted water to a boil. Add the rice and simmer for 35 minutes, stirring occasionally. During the last 2 minutes of cooking time, add the peas and the leek or asparagus, if using. Drain to remove excess water. Peel the mango and cut out as much flesh around the pit as you can. Cut mango into cubes. Chop your herbs of choice. Add mango and herbs to the rice. To make the dressing, wash the lemon in hot water, zest it, and juice it. Whisk together the lemon zest, lemon juice, olive oil, and maple syrup or other sweetener. Season with salt and pepper. Pour the dressing over the salad and toss.

TIP:

For a more substantial variation or to take on a picnic,
add pieces of mozzarella or feta, or mixed nuts.

MIE GOReNG

The best *mie goreng* I ever ate was in Bali.
I was there on a surfing trip and spent long days outdoors on the water
or on hiking trails. I stayed in a warung with a lovely
Indonesian family, and that's when I really came to appreciate this
energy-dense dish in all its delicious glory.

4 ½ OZ (125 G) ASIAN INSTANT NOODLES (SEE "TIP")
1 SMALL ONION
1–2 GARLIC CLOVES
1 RED CHILI PEPPER
¼ OZ (10 G) FRESH GINGER
2 TBSP CANOLA OIL
1 LEEK, 1 BELL PEPPER, 2 CARROTS
HANDFUL OR TWO OF SEASONED OR MARINATED SHRIMP, OR STRIPS OF COOKED CHICKEN BREAST, OR THINLY SLICED LEFTOVER STEAK
2 EGGS, 2 TBSP SOY SAUCE
2 TBSP HOT SAUCE (SUCH AS SRIRACHA)
SALT AND BLACK PEPPER
½ BUNCH CILANTRO

In a bowl, cover the noodles with boiling water (or cook the noodles according to the package instructions) and set aside.

Finely dice the onion and ginger. Mince the garlic. Thinly slice the chili and the leek. Julienne the carrots and bell pepper.

In a large wok or skillet, heat the oil. Add the onion, garlic, and chili, and sauté. Add the leek, bell pepper, and carrots, and sauté until cooked but still firm to the bite. Add the shrimp, chicken, or steak.

Drain the noodles and add them to the skillet, mixing to combine with the veggies. In a small bowl, whisk the eggs and add them to the skillet. Add the soy sauce, hot sauce, and salt and pepper to taste. Just before serving, chop and add the cilantro leaves to the noodles. Serve in small bowls, as they do in Indonesia.

TIP:

Most Asian noodles will work with this dish; try egg, rice, or ramen noodles.
Feel free to use vegetables other than the ones listed here; try baby spinach, bok choy, or zucchini.

QUICK RATATOUILLE

This Mediterranean classic is the definition of simplicity.
With enough layers of flavor to shine as a vegan entree in its own right,
it can also serve as a hearty side for fish or steak, a pasta sauce,
or to top a bowl of grains or rice. Vegetarians can add some richness by
sprinkling a handful of mozzarella cubes into the ratatouille
during the last five minutes of cooking.

---

1 ONION	Dice the onion, finely chop the garlic, and thinly slice the chili pepper, if using. Cut the eggplant, zucchini, and bell peppers into bite-sized pieces. Pick the rosemary and thyme leaves from the stems, and coarsely chop.
1–2 GARLIC CLOVES	
1 EGGPLANT	
1–2 ZUCCHINI	
2 RED OR YELLOW BELL PEPPERS	
1 SPRIG ROSEMARY	
1 SPRIG THYME	In a large pot, heat the oil. Add the onions, garlic, and chili, if using, and sauté until soft and translucent. Add the bell peppers and sauté for 1 more minute. Add the eggplant, zucchini, herbs, and tomato paste. Mix everything together well, then deglaze with the water. Add the sugar, season with salt and pepper, and cover. Stir again after 5 minutes, then remove from heat and let rest for several minutes before serving.
3 TBSP OLIVE OIL	
2 TBSP TOMATO PASTE	
¼ CUP (50 ML) WATER	
½ TSP SUGAR	
½ RED CHILI PEPPER (OPTIONAL)	
SALT AND BLACK PEPPER	

TIP:

You can replace the tomato paste and water with canned
chopped tomatoes (7 OZ / 200 G), or 3 fresh ripe tomatoes. Leftover ratatouille
doubles as a fabulous salad the next day, or it can be pureed and reimagined
as a spread for crostini or wraps. Make another batch right away!

MiNESTRONE

2 CARROTS, 2 STALKS CELERY
1 SMALL ZUCCHINI
2 WAXY POTATOES,
SUCH AS YUKON GOLD
½ ONION OR 1 SHALLOT
1 GARLIC CLOVE
2 TBSP OLIVE OR CANOLA OIL
2 TBSP TOMATO PASTE
½ TSP DRIED OREGANO
¼ CUP BASMATI RICE, RINSED
4–6 CUPS ORGANIC VEGETABLE STOCK
¼ CUP THIN NOODLES
½ BUNCH PARSLEY
SALT AND BLACK PEPPER
PESTO (SEE PAGE 26) AND/OR
GRATED PARMESAN
(OPTIONAL)

Dice the carrots, celery, zucchini, potatoes, and onion or shallot; crush the garlic. In a large pot, add the onion or shallot and the garlic, and sauté until soft and translucent. Stir in the tomato paste. Add the vegetables, potatoes, oregano, and rice, then pour in the stock. Bring to a boil, reduce heat to medium, and simmer for 5 minutes. Add the noodles and cook until al dente, about 5 minutes more.

Season to taste with salt and pepper. Ladle into bowls and garnish with chopped parsley leaves, a dollop of pesto, if using, and a sprinkle of parmesan. Alternatively, the pesto and parmesan can be served on the side.

Minestrone and fresh baguette slices are a match made in heaven.

TIP:

You can get creative with your choice of vegetables; as an example, cabbage (Chinese, savoy, or white) tastes good in this soup. You can also substitute pearl barley or another small grain for the Basmati rice, or add extra noodles.

RISOTTO

To this day, the best Italian cooks still argue about proper risotto technique: Is a good risotto to be (gently) shaken or stirred? To begin with, you need the right kind of short-grain rice: arborio, carnaroli, or vialone nano. Each variety calls for slightly different cooking times, and absorbs liquids a touch differently. My favorite is carnaroli; it produces a luxuriously creamy risotto, but remains pleasantly firm to the bite.

2 TBSP CANOLA OIL
½ ONION OR 1 SHALLOT
1 GARLIC CLOVE
1 CUP SHORT-GRAIN RISOTTO RICE
2 ½–3 ½ CUPS VEGETABLE STOCK
½ CUP (100 ML) WHITE WINE
(SAVE THE REST OF THE BOTTLE
FOR DRINKING!)
SALT AND BLACK PEPPER
1 TBSP UNSALTED BUTTER
GRATED PARMESAN OR
ANOTHER HARD CHEESE
CHOPPED HERBS (OPTIONAL)

Finely chop the onion and garlic. In a pot or deep pan, heat the oil. Add the onion, garlic, any extras you may be using cut into bite-sized pieces (see "Variations"), and sauté briefly. Add the rice and stir until all the kernels are shiny and coated with oil.

Add the wine, deglaze the pot, and lightly season with salt and pepper. Add 1 ladleful of stock. Let simmer until the rice has completely absorbed the liquid, then add another ladleful of stock. Every now and then, stir the rice or gently shake the pot. Turn off heat after 10–15 minutes (depending on the kind of rice you use) and cover the pot. Let the risotto stand for a few more minutes. (Do not transfer pot to a cold surface; you don't want any heat escaping.)

Just before serving, stir in the butter, the cheese, the herbs, if using, and season to taste with salt and pepper.

VARIATIONS

You can vary and refine the risotto by adding saffron, tomato paste, asparagus, mushrooms, or seafood, to name a few options. And just before serving, stir in your choice of fresh herbs!

POLENTA

4 CUPS ORGANIC
VEGETABLE STOCK OR WATER
1 CUP POLENTA
GRATED PARMESAN
1 TBSP UNSALTED BUTTER

In a pot, add the stock or water and bring to a boil. (If using water, add 2 teaspoons salt.) Stirring constantly, slowly add the polenta. Reduce heat to low and continue stirring until the polenta thickens, about 10-15 minutes. Stir in the Parmesan and the butter, and serve. For an even creamier, smoother polenta, substitute milk for the stock or water in this basic recipe.

VARIATIONS

MUSHROOM POLENTA:
In a pot, heat 1 tablespoon olive oil. Add 10 thinly sliced button or cremini mushrooms, 1 tablespoon diced onions, and 1 peeled and chopped clove of garlic. Sauté until the onions are soft and translucent then pour in the stock or water. Bring to a boil, add the polenta, and proceed with the basic recipe.

RED WINE POLENTA:
Replace the stock, water, or milk with 1 cup red wine and 2 tablespoons thinly sliced radicchio.

SAFFRON POLENTA:
Add a generous pinch of ground saffron to the hot liquid.

TRUFFLED POLENTA:
Just before serving, stir in some truffle oil or truffle butter.

SWEET POLENTA:
Cook the polenta in 2 cups water plus 2 cups milk. Sweeten to taste with brown sugar or honey; add a pinch or two of cinnamon, if you wish. This variation is delicious with caramelized plum compote (page 31).

TIP:
Smooth any leftover polenta on a plate or cutting board and let it cool, uncovered. Cut the polenta into pieces. In a skillet, heat 1 tablespoon olive oil and cook the polenta until golden brown on all sides. You can also add a beaten egg yolk into the skillet towards the end. Fried polenta is a great side dish for beef.

SPINACH AND CHEESE DUMPLINGS

These hearty dumplings originate in the mountain farmhouses of South Tyrol, so I'd recommend using a flavorful Gruyère or other Alpine cheese to make them.

1 ONION
1 GARLIC CLOVE
1 TBSP UNSALTED BUTTER
9 OZ (250 G) DAY-OLD WHITE BREAD, BREAD ROLLS, OR BAGUETTE
1 CUP HOT MILK
3 EGGS
2-3 HANDFULS FRESH SPINACH
5 ½ OZ (150 G) GRUYÈRE OR AGED GOUDA
GROUND NUTMEG
SALT AND BLACK PEPPER
½ BUNCH PARSLEY

Dice the onion, chop the garlic, and coarsely chop the spinach. In a large skillet, heat the butter. Cook the onions and garlic until soft and translucent. Add the spinach, and cook until it begins to wilt.

Slice or cube the bread and transfer it to a big bowl. Pour in the hot milk. Let stand for about 15 minutes. Add the spinach mixture to the bread, and season to taste with nutmeg, salt and pepper. Cut the cheese into small cubes. In a separate bowl, beat the eggs. Add the beaten eggs and the cheese to the bread mixture, and mix well to combine. If the mixture is too wet, add some breadcrumbs; if it is too dry, add a splash of milk.

Bring a large pot of water with ½ teaspoon salt to boil. Moisten your hands with water, and shape dough into small dumplings. Cook the dumplings in the boiling water over medium heat for 5 minutes. Reduce heat to low, and cook the dumplings for about 10 minutes more. The dumplings are ready when they rise to the top and turn over on their own. Remove with a slotted spoon, sprinkle with freshly chopped parsley, and serve.

TIP:

In a skillet, heat some butter. Add a handful of breadcrumbs and cook until golden brown. Scatter over the dumplings and serve.

Leftover dumplings can be sliced and browned in a skillet with a bit of olive oil.

ASIAN STIR-FRY WITH MILLET and VEGETABLES

Yogurt-lemon dip (page 87) goes very well with this dish.
Leftover stir-fry tastes delicious cold, so it's another good option
for the road or the trail.

2 CARROTS
2 SMALL ZUCCHINI
½ ONION OR 1 SHALLOT
1 GARLIC CLOVE
2 TBSP OLIVE OR CANOLA OIL
½ TSP TURMERIC
½ TSP RAS EL HANOUT
1 CUP MILLET
1-2 CUPS ORGANIC VEGETABLE STOCK
½ BUNCH PARSLEY
OR CILANTRO
HANDFUL OF PITTED DATES
OR RAISINS
ZEST AND JUICE OF 1 ORGANIC ORANGE
SALT AND BLACK PEPPER
CHILI FLAKES
YOGURT-LEMON DIP

Dice the onion or shallot, the carrots, and the zucchini. Mince the garlic. In a pot, heat the oil. Add the onion or shallot and the garlic, and cook until soft and translucent. Add the turmeric, ras el hanout, and millet into the pot. Little by little, pour in the vegetable stock. Simmer until the millet is almost cooked, then add the carrots and zucchini and continue to simmer until the vegetables start to soften.

Mix in the dates or raisins and the orange zest and juice. Chop the parsley or cilantro leaves and add them to the stir-fry. Season to taste with salt, pepper, and chili flakes, and serve with a dollop of yogurt-lemon dip.

TIP:

You can mix and match the vegetables; try squash, leeks, and/or bell peppers.
You can also try using quinoa instead of millet.

144

MOUNTAIN BIKING

PURE FLOW

Hardly any other sport gives you the feeling of flow like mountain biking does. It doesn't matter one bit whether you ride on hidden trails up the mountain slopes under your own steam, or whether you take a lift up to a network of trails you can then ride down. Any way you choose to have fun has its own appeal.

When I tell people I come from Oberammergau, most of them think of woodcarvers, the world-famous Passion Play, and Linderhof Palace, the favorite residence of Ludwig II, the Bavarian "Fairytale King." But the Oberammergau area has so much more to offer. There are relatively easy hiking trails in the foothills of the Alps, with breathtaking panoramic views all the way to Munich and Lake Starnberg, or enticing hiking routes in the area around the Zugspitze massif all the way deep into the Tyrolean mountains. Teeming with demanding steep slopes, bike trails, and climbing opportunities, the mountain world around O'gau (what locals call Oberammergau) has a great deal to offer. And, yes, there are plenty of beer gardens for replenishing those lost electrolytes afterwards.

In a bike park, you can really let your soul chill. The atmosphere is relaxed; there are routes for every experience level, long opening hours, a bar, and a small shop to fulfil every need. Of course, you can also rent a bike or test one out if you haven't brought yours along. Bike parks offer courses, training, and guided tours.

LUKAS GERUM

MARKUS REISER

Two well-known faces in the mountain-biking scene—Markus Reiser and Lukas Gerum—run the newly redesigned "Focus Bikepark" in Oberammergau. Markus is still active in the Enduro World Series and has had many successes, including international ones. Lukas has ridden right up at the front in marathon and cross-country races in Germany. The two very likeable Oberammergau natives share more than a love of mountain biking and the bike park; they share a long friendship.

I got to know Lukas a few years ago, when I was freeriding in winter. I have seldom met a more cheerful person. Since then, we have had many a mountain adventure together. In critical situations, Lukas is the definition of calm. With an ever-present, genuine smile on his face, he sees the bright side in everything. Our deep philosophical discussions at night, around the campfire, stay with me long afterwards.

HOW MANY DAYS A YEAR DO YOU SPEND OUTDOORS?

Lukas: Certainly over 200 days. During the summer, we are either in the forest building trails or riding. In the winter I often go ski touring.
Markus: Since I cycle professionally, I am away often, and gladly. I definitely spend 30 weekends a year outdoors.

DURING YOUR TRIPS, WHAT ARE YOUR FAVORITE DISHES THAT YOU MAKE YOURSELF?

Lukas: When I'm traveling I usually cook with an excessive amount of garlic, and my favorite dish with garlic is gnocchi.

Markus: If it has to be fast, I always have a can of chickpeas with me. I warm them up quickly in a pan and pep them up by adding an egg and good spices like turmeric and chili. In 5 minutes I have fortified myself for an active day outdoors.

WHAT DO YOU EAT TO GIVE YOURSELVES ENERGY BEFORE AND AFTER A TIRING RACE, OR ON A LONG AND PARTICULARLY CHALLENGING TRIP?

Lukas: Depending on where I am at the time, I try to eat whatever is typical of that region. Before and during the trip I like something sweet.
Markus: At the moment, quinoa with fresh vegetables and a flavorful sauce is my favorite meal before a race. There are certainly some good inspirations in your book. I usually eat dried fruit at the finish line, which gives me quick energy.

Dining out

COOKING OUTDOORS ON THE BARBECUE
AND THE CAMPFIRE

What a beautiful summer evening! The smiling sun is giving way to a
sliver of a moon. There is no better time to get the grill going or light a campfire
and enjoy a meal under the stars. These moments are priceless—setting up
the tables and chairs outside, often with a view of the sea or mountains that no
restaurant can offer, breaking bread with a group of friends. In this section,
you will find recipes that are made to be cooked outside and shared.
You will also find practical tips and tricks for making the most of outdoor cooking.

LIGHT MY FIRE

CAMPFIRE TIPS

Making a fire was once fundamental for surviving in nature, and it still has a magical, irresistible quality for humans today. A crackling campfire invites one to dream, to feel safe and protected. It warms, dries, illuminates, grills, bakes. But, predictably, in many areas it is now forbidden to build an open fire; the risk of it getting out of control and developing into a devastating forest fire is often too great. So do your research beforehand: find out whether campfires are allowed, and if so, precisely where. See the next page for some pointers on building a campfire safely, quickly, and effectively—so that it doesn't just smoke and go out right away.

1.
PICKING A SITE FOR THE FIRE

Your site should be in an area sheltered from the wind, and far away from flammable materials, such as thin branches or dry leaves. A gravel riverbed, sandy soil, or hard rocky surfaces are good. If you are in a forested area, remove all flammable materials from the site until you see bare earth. Build a pit, or place green branches underneath.

2.
PREPARING THE FIRE PIT

First, check whether there is an old campfire site nearby that you can use. If not, dig or scrape out a shallow pit about 4 in (10 cm) deep and 20 in (50 cm) wide and/or build a ring of rocks around it. This is for safety, but it also makes placing a cooking grate over the fire easier.

3.
GATHERING TINDER, KINDLING, AND FIREWOOD

Dry tinder is the most important thing you need to get a fire going. You can use dry grasses, tree bark, small pinecones, or dry leaves, among others. You will also need kindling (twigs and thin branches that serve to "transfer" flames from tinder to wood), and large pieces of firewood. Again, planning ahead is key. Once it gets dark it will be much harder to find firewood, not to mention you should never leave your fire unattended and go search for wood. Be on the lookout, also, for animals (some of them poisonous) hiding in dry woodpiles or dead wood when collecting kindling and firewood. Lastly, gather only dry branches and fallen wood. Don't chop down anything healthy or green; it won't burn well anyways.

4.
BUILDING AND LIGHTING A FIRE

Loosely pile your tinder in the middle of the fire pit. Arrange a tent of thin branches (your kindling) over the tinder. Light the fire and carefully blow air into it. To light the fire, a lighter or matches will do, but you can also use a FireSteel. When you strike the FireSteel with the back of your knife, hot sparks shoot out; it makes you feel like a trapper! Made of magnesium alloy, FireSteels are weatherproof, inexpensive, and easily available wherever camping gear is sold. As soon as there are small flames in your nest of tinder, slowly add thicker and thicker branches to your kindling tent. Don't rush your fire; give it enough time and air to grow, blowing into it a few times if necessary.

Push the longer, thicker branches into the fire as they burn, or cut them into pieces beforehand with a saw (I always carry a folding wood saw with me).

5.
CONTROLLING AND EXTINGUISHING A FIRE

Do not let your fire get too big, and always keep an eye out for flying sparks. Before going to bed or hitting the road, extinguish the fire completely (ideally with water, dirt, or sand). If you have leftover wood, pile it up near the fire pit. Whoever comes next will be very happy to have it!

VEGETABLE ANTIPASTI

2 BELL PEPPERS
2 SMALL ZUCCHINI
1 EGGPLANT
1 GARLIC CLOVE
1 TBSP OLIVE OIL
FRESH HERBS (SUCH AS THYME,
ROSEMARY, OR PARSLEY)
SALT AND BLACK PEPPER
CHILI POWDER

Cut the vegetables into sticks or bite-sized pieces. Mince the garlic. Separate the leaves from the stems of the herbs; coarsely chop the leaves.

To cook on the grill:
There are two methods. You can put the uncooked vegetables in a bowl, add the garlic, olive oil, and chopped herbs, and season to taste with salt and pepper. Leave to marinate briefly, then grill the vegetables over high heat until charred on both sides, about 1-2 minutes per side. Or, you can marinate each vegetable separately after grilling. Grill the vegetables over high heat until charred on both sides, about 1-2 minutes per side. Transfer each type of vegetable to a separate bowl or deep platter. Sprinkle in your choice of chopped herbs and season to taste with salt and pepper. Drizzle with a bit of olive oil and let marinate. For example, try the peppers with rosemary, the zucchini with thyme, and the eggplant with parsley.

To cook on the stove:
The same choice applies here: marinate the vegetables either before or after cooking. (If you marinate before, note that you will need less olive oil for cooking.) To cook, add some olive oil to a skillet and heat. Working in small batches, cook each type of vegetable separately until tender, adding more oil as needed.

Again, feel free to use other types of vegetables: squash, carrot, leek, and fennel all make beautiful antipasti. You can also get creative with the seasonings.

TIP:
Marinate the eggplant in 1 tablespoon honey and
1 teaspoon ras el hanout along with the garlic, olive oil, and herbs.
Cook, garnish with chopped walnuts, and serve.

Use leftover antipasti to make a
mouthwatering sandwich or wrap.

THE **BEST**
BURGER EVER

Burgers have made an impressive comeback into the restaurant mainstream, and they are riding a wave of hype and popularity. Though fast-food classics, burgers can easily be transformed into healthier versions without sacrificing any of the flavor. Baking your own hamburger buns (page 25) makes a huge difference. When you taste ground beef patties grilled over charcoal or an open fire, you will see burgers in a whole new light. High-quality ingredients, good cheese, and your own creativity will make your hamburgers truly stand out.

BACON CHEESE BURGER

2 BURGER BUNS (PAGE 25)

PATTIES
10 OZ (300 G) GROUND BEEF
½ TSP EACH SALT AND BLACK PEPPER

TOPPINGS
½ ENGLISH CUCUMBER
1 TOMATO
1 DILL PICKLE
2 SLICES CHEESE,
SUCH AS GOUDA OR GRUYÈRE
4 SLICES BACON
2 SALAD LEAVES
1 TSP MUSTARD
2 TSP KETCHUP
1 TSP MAYONNAISE
SLICED ONIONS
FRESH WATERCRESS
(OPTIONAL)

Preheat the grill. Season the ground meat with salt and pepper. Using your hands, knead to combine. Moisten your hands with water, and form two patties. They will shrink as they cook, so make the patties slightly bigger than the buns. Slice the cucumber, tomato, and dill pickle.

In a skillet, cook the bacon until crisp. Cook the onions according to preference: sauté them in the bacon fat until they are soft and translucent, grill them, or just leave them raw.

Grill the patties until nicely browned on one side, about 3 minutes. Flip, top each patty with a slice of cheese, and grill for another 2-3 minutes. Slice the burger buns in half and grill them cut-side down.

Place the patties on the buns, layer to taste with the remaining ingredients, and enjoy!

VARIATIONS

BIG KAHUNA BURGER

Add 2 tablespoons of soy or teriyaki sauce to the ground beef.
When you flip the patties, top them with a slice of pineapple each,
then cover with a slice of cheese.

VEGGIE

Replace the beef patties
with falafel (page 84).

BIG ITALIAN BURGER

Add a bit of chopped rosemary and minced garlic to the ground beef.
Replace the cucumber with grilled vegetable antipasti (page 160),
smoked bacon with prosciutto, and gruyère or gouda with Taleggio.
Use arugula instead of watercress.

TAGLIATA

STEAK PERFECTION

1 LARGE BEEF STEAK
7–9 OZ (200–250 G) PER PERSON
SALT AND BLACK PEPPER
OLIVE OIL, LEMON JUICE, AND HERBS

The choice of steak is very important. If possible, source it from a good butcher. Ask for marbled, aged meat, and choose cuts like flank steak, ribeye, porterhouse, or T-bone. You definitely want to leave large, thick steaks whole to share with someone.

Take your steak out of the cooler bag 1–2 hours before grilling, to bring it to room temperature. Leave the meat in its packaging, and keep it out of the sun!

Arrange the wood or coals in such a way that you have a corner free of coals or wood to use as a resting zone.

Season the steak lightly with salt. Place it on the grill, and brown it over high heat on both sides. Then, grill the steak over a lower heat. If needed, move the steak to the resting zone. Use the finger test (page 173) to check your steak for doneness.
Steak tastes best when it is cooked medium rare or medium. When the steak releases red to pink juices, wrap it in foil and set it aside in the resting zone for 5 minutes.

Transfer steak to a cutting board, and slice against the grain into thick slices. Season generously with salt and pepper. Give it a drizzle of olive oil, a squeeze of lemon, and a sprinkle of herbs.

TIP:
Ratatouille, polenta, sweet potatoes, baked potatoes, or just a fresh baguette will accompany the tagliata perfectly.

If you have any leftovers, they will make a very special sandwich indeed.

THE FINGER TEST

HOW TO CHECK THE DONENESS OF MEAT

1.

Hold one hand out, palm open and relaxed, facing up. Gently press the index finger of your other hand on the ball of your thumb (the soft, fleshy part between the base of your thumb and your wrist). This is how steak feels when it's raw.

2.

On your open hand, touch your index finger to the tip of your thumb, forming an "O." Press the index finger of your other hand on the ball of your thumb, which should feel a bit harder now. This is how steak feels when it's rare (bloody).

3.

Move to the next finger. On your open hand, touch your middle finger on the tip of your thumb, forming an "O." Press the index finger of your other hand on the ball of your thumb. This is how steak feels when it's medium rare (between pink and red). My favorite!

4.

Keep moving to your next finger. On your open hand, touch your ring finger to the tip of your thumb. Press the index finger of your other hand on the ball of your thumb. It should feel harder still. This is how steak feels when it's medium (pink inside, but not bloody). Most people like their steak cooked this way.

5.

Lastly, on your open finger, touch your pinky to the tip of your thumb. Press the index finger of your other hand on the ball of your thumb, which should be very taut. This is how steak feels when it's well-done.

NOTE:

Compare by pressing on the steak with your finger or the barbecue tongs. When it feels like it has reached your preferred doneness, remove steak from the grill.

COD FILLETS
WITH AN OAT CRUST

If cod is not available, use any other firm-fleshed white fish.

2 COD FILLETS,
EACH 5–7 OZ (150–200 G)
3 TBSP ALL-PURPOSE FLOUR
1 CUP ROLLED OATS
1 EGG
2 TBSP LEMON JUICE
2 TBSP CANOLA OIL
HUNGARIAN PAPRIKA
SALT AND BLACK PEPPER
1 TSP UNSALTED BUTTER
LEMON WEDGES

Lay the cod fillets flat on a plate. In two separate plates, put the flour and the rolled oats. In a bowl, beat the egg with 1 tablespoon of water or milk. Drizzle the fillets with lemon juice, and season with paprika, salt, and pepper. Dredge both sides of the fillets in the flour and shake off the excess. Then, using a fork to avoid sticky fingers, dip both sides of the fillets in the egg. Lastly, dip each fillet in the rolled oats, turning several times and pressing down lightly to coat evenly.

In a skillet or frying pan, heat the oil over medium heat. Add the fish and cook until the breading turns golden brown and the fish is cooked through. Reduce heat to low, add 1 tablespoon of butter to the pan, and let it foam. Using a spoon, baste the pieces of fish with foaming butter. This makes them taste especially delicious. Serve with lemon wedges.

Crusted fish fillets also pair well with simple salads, like a cucumber or a potato salad.

TIP:
Try using this oat crust with chicken, too,
or other types of fish fillets, like pike.

For a VEGETARIAN version, you can replace the fish with
halloumi or feta cheese, or thinly sliced celery root.

HOW TO FILLET A FISH

Whether you caught the fish yourself or bought it fresh at the market, filleting is not a hard skill to master. It's a must for every outdoor cook; all it takes is a bit of practice.

Besides the fish, you will need a really sharp knife—ideally a light and flexible one. If you don't own a special fish-filleting knife, choose a knife with a blade as long and thin as possible. You will also need a cutting board or another clean, non-slip surface.

1.
SCALING:

First, determine whether or not you need to scale the fish; you may plan to cook the filleted fish without the skin, or use fish like trout or char, which don't need scaling at all. I love crispy fried skin, since it protects the fillet from drying out when you cook it. To scale fish you can use a special fish scaler, but a knife or a sturdy tablespoon will also do nicely. Hold the fish by the tail. With the back of your knife, start scraping against the scales from tail to head. Work until all scales come off and the fish feels smooth.

2.
GUTTING AND CLEANING:

Insert the tip of your knife into the underside of the fish, and slide it from the anus up to the bottom of the gills. Be careful not to cut too deeply; if you puncture the gallbladder (just below the head), the fish will be ruined. Next, open the cavity and carefully remove the entrails. If needed, cut through the gullet. Using a teaspoon, scrape out the black vein along the spine. Wash the fish well inside and out, and pat dry.

3.
FILLETING:

Lay the fish down flat. Angling the knife towards the head, make a slightly curved cut just behind the gills on one side of the fish. Flip the knife horizontally. With the blade facing the tail, cut the fish along the spine down towards the tail. Then, lift up the fillet and carefully cut it free from the body with smooth strokes; you may have to cut through strong fish bones. Repeat with the second fillet. Now, all that's left is to take out the small bones in the cavity wall, slice off the fins, and trim the fillets. All set!

If you want to remove all the fish bones cleanly, use the back of the knife to scrape once along the fillet from tail to head. This will make the pin bones stand up, so you can pick them out with tweezers or needle-nose pliers.

FIRE BARREL CHEESE FONDUE

The idea for this convivial outdoor fondue came about on cold winter nights in the mountains, surrounded by deep snow. After a long day backcountry skiing, sitting by a crackling fire in front of the van is the ultimate comfort. To expedite the building of a fire, a friend made a small fire barrel that you can also cook on. The stage for an outdoor fondue is set! Of course, you can make the fondue just as easily in a Dutch oven on a grate over a fire (see also page 189), or on stovetop inside the van, if the weather is severe. The bottom line is that whoever drops a piece of bread in the fondue has to clean up afterwards!

7 OZ (200 G) EACH GRUYÈRE
AND GOUDA (OR EMMENTAL) CHEESE
½ LOAF DARK FARMER'S BREAD
OR 1 LOAF CRUSTY WHITE BREAD
1 CUP WHITE WINE
PINCH OF GRATED NUTMEG
WHITE PEPPER OR
GROUND CAYENNE PEPPER
1 GARLIC CLOVE (OPTIONAL)
1 SHOT GLASS FRUIT BRANDY (OPTIONAL)

Coarsely grate the cheese. Cut the bread into
bite-sized pieces. If using, cut the garlic clove
in half and rub the inside of the pot with it.
In a pot over very low heat, pour half of the
wine. Add the cheese, stirring constantly until
it is melted. While stirring, add the remaining
wine, the nutmeg, and the white or cayenne
pepper. Stir in the fruit brandy, if using.

The cheese must be melted, but not piping hot, or
it will burn the tongue. Spear a bread cube with
a fork or, even better, whittle a thin branch to
a point for a makeshift fondue fork. Dunk bread
into the melted cheese and turn to coat.

FLATBREAD GRILLED ON A STONE

2 CUPS ALL-PURPOSE FLOUR, SPELT FLOUR, OR LIGHT WHOLE WHEAT FLOUR, ½ TSP SALT, 1 TBSP CANOLA OR OLIVE OIL, ½ CUP WATER, 2 TBSP MELTED UNSALTED BUTTER

In a bowl, place the flour and the salt. Add the oil and water a little bit at a time, and knead to form a smooth dough. Cover and let rest for about 15 minutes.

Shape the dough into a roll and divide into 10-12 pieces. Sprinkle lightly with flour. Using a rolling pin or a clean wine bottle, roll out each piece into a flat disk approximately 6 inches (15 cm) in diameter.

Heat a flat stone over the campfire, then move it to the edge of your fire pit. Place each flatbread on the stone and grill briefly on both sides. Brush the tops of the cooked flatbreads with butter and pile on a plate for serving. You can also use a cast-iron or other skillet, instead of the stone, for cooking the flatbreads.

TIP:

I really love the dips on pages 86-87 with this flatbread. Served with chicken skewers or kebabs, the flatbread makes a simple, yet very special, amazingly delicious outdoor meal.

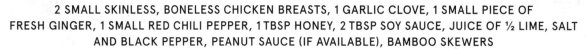

CHICKEN SATAY

2 SMALL SKINLESS, BONELESS CHICKEN BREASTS, 1 GARLIC CLOVE, 1 SMALL PIECE OF FRESH GINGER, 1 SMALL RED CHILI PEPPER, 1 TBSP HONEY, 2 TBSP SOY SAUCE, JUICE OF ½ LIME, SALT AND BLACK PEPPER, PEANUT SAUCE (IF AVAILABLE), BAMBOO SKEWERS

Soak the skewers in water. Cut the chicken breast lengthwise into thin strips. Make the marinade: Mince the garlic and ginger and put them in a bowl. Thinly slice the chili pepper and add it to the bowl. Add the honey, soy sauce, and lime juice, and stir to combine. Season to taste with salt and pepper. Add the chicken strips and toss to coat with the marinade. Ideally, marinate chicken in the refrigerator for a few hours or overnight; otherwise, cook straightaway. Thread the chicken onto skewers, leave one third of each skewer free at the end.

Grill over medium heat until the chicken is well-browned on both sides and cooked through. Serve with peanut sauce, if available, on the side.

ADANA KEBAB

1-2 GARLIC CLOVES, 1 ONION, 10 OZ (300 G) GROUND BEEF, 1 TSP HUNGARIAN PAPRIKA, 1 TSP GROUND CUMIN OR RAS EL HANOUT, SALT AND BLACK PEPPER, CHILI POWDER, 2 TSP FRESHLY CHOPPED THYME, FLATBREAD AND YOGURT-LEMON DIP (PAGE 87), 4 SKEWERS

Finely dice the onion; mince the garlic. In a bowl add the beef, onion, garlic, paprika, cumin, chili, thyme, salt, and pepper. Knead well to combine. Divide the mixture into 4 pieces. Take a skewer (metal or wood, or a trimmed fresh long willow branch) and form a hotdog-sized kebab around it, pressing firmly. Grill the kebabs until nicely charred. Tuck into flatbreads and serve with yogurt-lemon dip.

ADANA KEBAB

CHICKEN SATAY

LAMB SHAWARMA

10 OZ (300 G) SADDLE OF LAMB, DEBONED

MARINADE
3 TBSP YOGURT
2 TBSP OLIVE OIL
½ TSP GROUND CUMIN
1 GARLIC CLOVE
1 SMALL RED CHILI PEPPER
PINCH OF CINNAMON
JUICE OF ½ LEMON

TOPPING
2 SPRIGS PARSLEY
½ ENGLISH CUCUMBER
1 TOMATO
1 SMALL ONION
SALT AND BLACK PEPPER
HUMMUS OR YOGURT-LEMON DIP
(PAGES 86–87)
2 LARGE TORTILLAS OR 1 PITA

Make the marinade: Mince the garlic; finely chop the chili. Combine all marinade ingredients and pour them into a large freezer bag. Add the lamb and turn to coat with marinade. Seal the bag and marinate lamb in the refrigerator, ideally overnight.

Remove the lamb from the bag and pat it dry. Reserve the marinade. Sear both sides of the lamb on the grill, then move it to the edge and cook slowly for about 5 minutes more, brushing with reserved marinade a few times as it cooks. Remove lamb from the grill and cut into thin slices.

Dice the tomato and cucumber, thinly slice the onion, and coarsely chop the parsley. On the grill, briefly warm the tortillas or the pita cut in half. Season the lamb with salt and pepper and divide it, together with the toppings, between the tortillas or pita halves. If using tortillas, roll them into a wrap (see page 91 for how to make a tortilla wrap).

FRIED SWEET POTATOES WITH ASPARAGUS

While this recipe was developed for a skillet or frying pan, the vegetables can be grilled instead. If you choose to grill them, cut the sweet potatoes into thicker slices, and cut the asparagus in half. A fantastic vegetarian dish on its own, it also adds flavor and a splash of vivid color to any grilled fish or meat dish.

2–3 SWEET POTATOES
1 SMALL BUNCH ASPARAGUS, WHITE OR GREEN
½ BUNCH SCALLIONS
½ BUNCH PARSLEY OR CILANTRO
4 TBSP OLIVE OIL
SALT AND BLACK PEPPER
CHILI POWDER
1 GARLIC CLOVE AND
THE JUICE OF ½ LEMON (OPTIONAL)

Peel the sweet potato and cut it into thin slices. Trim the tough ends off the asparagus and cut into pieces about 1½ in (4 cm) long. Thinly slice the scallions and chop the herbs. Mince the garlic, if using. In a bowl, combine the olive oil, herbs, and garlic and lemon juice, if using. Season to taste with salt, pepper, and chili powder. Add the vegetables, toss well to coat, and let marinate. Heat a skillet and add the sweet potato first. Cook until browned on both sides. Repeat with the asparagus. (If grilling, place vegetables on a hot grill until nicely charred.) Transfer vegetables to a bowl, toss with more herbs, scatter the scallions on top, and serve.

Yogurt-lemon dip (page 87) tastes very good with this dish.

BAKED POTATOES WITH HERBED FRESH CHEESE

4 LARGE RUSSET POTATOES
2 TBSP OLIVE OIL
2 GARLIC CLOVES
1 CUP FULL-FAT SOUR CREAM
(OR QUARK WITH 20% FAT, IF AVAILABLE)
1 CUP LIGHT SOUR CREAM
(OR REGULAR QUARK, IF AVAILABLE)
½ CUP MILK
FRESH HERBS
(SUCH AS PARSLEY, BASIL,
DILL, CHERVIL, CILANTRO)
SALT AND BLACK PEPPER
CHILI POWDER OR
HUNGARIAN PAPRIKA

Wash and scrub the potatoes, but do not peel them. Place them on a large piece of aluminum foil. Drizzle with olive oil and sprinkle generously with salt on all sides. Wrap the potatoes up well. Ideally, bake the potatoes slow and low; meaning, for about 1 hour at the edge of the campfire, or in the resting zone of a charcoal barbecue. If the potatoes are precooked, reduce the cooking time by about half. Meanwhile, place the sour cream in a bowl. Stir in just enough milk so that the mixture is smooth and creamy, but not runny. Season to taste. Mince the garlic and add it to the bowl. Coarsely chop the herbs, leaves only, and add them to the bowl. Sprinkle with chili powder or paprika. Test the potatoes for doneness and serve with a dollop or two of herbed cheese topping. (You can also use other vegetables: try wrapping large pieces of squash, whole unpeeled beets, or whole fennel in aluminum foil.)

TIP:

Potatoes cook faster when they are precooked in boiling water for 15 minutes and cooled before baking. Foragers, use wild herbs (watercress, nettles, or oregano) instead.

BAKED VEGETABLES WITH FETA CHEESE

2 BELL PEPPERS
OR SWEET BANANA PEPPERS
2 ZUCCHINI
1 TBSP OLIVE OIL
5 ½ OZ (150 G) FETA CHEESE
FRESH HERBS,
SUCH AS ROSEMARY OR THYME
SALT AND BLACK PEPPER
1 RED CHILI PEPPER (OPTIONAL)

Cut the peppers and the zucchini into thick slices, and spread them on a piece of aluminum foil. Drizzle with the olive oil and season with salt and pepper. Coarsely crumble the feta over the vegetables, then add the herbs and the fresh chili pepper, sliced thinly, if using. Fold up the edges of the aluminum foil snugly around the vegetables to make a package.

Bake the vegetables for about 15 minutes, preferably at the edge of your campfire or in the resting zone of a charcoal barbecue. Test for doneness using a knife or a skewer. You can use other vegetables in lieu of the bell peppers and zucchini; try mushrooms, leeks, or eggplant.

TIP:

When I have some of my homemade pesto with me in the van, I marinate the feta in it before adding it to the vegetables.

MEDITERRANEAN CHICKEN STEW

1 BELL PEPPER
1 ZUCCHINI
1 RED OR WHITE ONION
1 MILD RED CHILI PEPPER
OR ½ TSP CHILI POWDER
2 GARLIC CLOVES
4 WAXY POTATOES, SUCH AS YUKON GOLD
2 WHOLE CHICKEN LEGS
4 TBSP OLIVE OIL
14 OZ (400 G) CANNED CHOPPED TOMATOES
½ CUP (100 ML) WINE (OPTIONAL)
SAFFRON POWDER OR TURMERIC
2 ½ – 3 OZ (70 – 100 G) DRAINED OLIVES
1 HANDFUL OF FRESH HERBS,
PREFERABLY ROSEMARY, THYME,
AND PARSLEY
HUNGARIAN PAPRIKA
SALT AND BLACK PEPPER

Cut the bell pepper and the zucchini into bite-sized pieces. Dice the onion and chili pepper, and mince the garlic. Peel and quarter the potatoes.

Generously season the chicken with salt, pepper, and paprika. Heat the olive oil in a Dutch oven or a large pot. Add the chicken legs and brown them on all sides. Remove the chicken from the pot and set aside. In the same pot, sauté the onion, garlic, and chili briefly. Add the bell pepper, the zucchini, and the chopped tomatoes, and pour in the wine, if using. Add the saffron or turmeric, and stir well.

Return the chicken legs to the pot and add the potatoes. Cover the pot and place it at the edge of the fire or over a low flame on the camp stove. Bring the chicken and vegetables to a boil, then cook at a bare simmer for about 45 minutes.

During the last 15 minutes of cooking time, add the olives. A couple of minutes before the end of cooking time, chop the herbs and scatter them into the pot. Season to taste with additional salt and pepper, if needed.

This stew is most delicious served with fresh baguette and a glass of wine.

TIP:
Leftover stew? Pull the chicken meat off the bones, chop it or shred it, and return it to the sauce.
Serve it over a luscious bowl of pasta and enjoy all over again!

DUTCH OVEN

A Dutch oven is made for boiling, braising, roasting, and baking—much
like in the Old West. Admittedly, this heavy cast-iron vessel is not designed for
tent camping or for a small van stove; a Dutch oven belongs outside,
over an open fire. And it is so versatile, you can even place glowing coals or
pieces of wood on the lid, for excellent bakes or braises. Of course, if
you can't make a fire, it goes without saying that you can cook beautifully
with your Dutch oven on a gas stove.

I own a set of five pots of different sizes. A lid lifter and a
three-legged stand are indispensable; you can also hang the Dutch oven on a hook
over the fire. To clean your Dutch oven, use only a brush, cloth, or sponge.
If you must use water, use plain water only—never any dishwashing soap.
Afterwards, to prevent it from rusting, let it dry and season it inside and out
with oil, just like you would a cast-iron skillet.

GRILLING A WHOLE FISH

It is actually quite easy to grill a whole fish. Just pay attention to a few specific things, and your success (not to mention a first-class flavor experience) is guaranteed. Whether freshwater or saltwater, the main thing to look for in fish is fairly firm, somewhat fatty flesh. Trout, pike, and eel, as well as sea bream, mackerel, and freshwater bream, are all good for the grill.

1–2 FISH, DEPENDING ON THEIR SIZE
½ ORGANIC LEMON
1 TSP UNSALTED BUTTER
½ BUNCH PARSLEY, THYME, OR ROSEMARY
1 TSP OLIVE OIL
SALT AND BLACK PEPPER
1 GARLIC CLOVE

Thoroughly rinse the fish and pat it dry. Season the cavity generously with salt and pepper. Slice the lemon into wedges and squeeze lightly over the fish. Place the butter and the herbs into the cavity. If using garlic, crush the unpeeled clove with a knife, cut it in half, and add it to the cavity. Just before grilling, rub the outside of the fish with olive oil, and season with salt and pepper.

YOU NOW HAVE SEVERAL OPTIONS

There are special baskets for grilling fish. A basket prevents the filling from spilling out, makes the fish easy to turn, and stops it from falling apart. For these reasons, a special grilling basket is always my first choice. If you don't have one, close up the cavity with a toothpick or a small twig, and place the fish gently on the grill. Or, the third option is to wrap the fish in heavy-duty aluminum foil, in which case you don't even really need a grate.

ALWAYS KEEP IN MIND

Never grill the fish over too-high heat, and keep it far enough from the heat to prevent it from charring on the outside but staying raw on the inside. Also, never leave the fish on the grill for too long, or it will dry out. Very fresh fish can still be slightly translucent after it is cooked. For example, a small trout or a sea bream only needs about 15 minutes on the grill.

TIP:

If you can pull out the fins at the top of the fish easily, the fish is done.

HOW TO KNOW IF A FISH IS FRESH

When buying a whole fish, you can quickly tell if it is freshly caught or if it has sat around for a while waiting for a buyer.

1.
Eyes: They should be clear and slightly bulging. Cloudy or sunken eyes mean the fish is no good; don't buy it!

2.
Gills: They should be light pink in color and appetizingly fresh. Darker or purple-colored gills indicate that the fish is not that fresh.

3.
Flesh: It should feel firm and elastic to the touch. If the flesh is soft and does not spring back when you press it, the fish is past its prime. Be wary!

4.
Smell: It should be mild, like the smell of the sea, and not fishy. This is how trained noses determine the freshness of fish.

SALTIMBOCCA

Italian Veal Schnitzels

4 SMALL VEAL CUTLETS, POUNDED VERY THIN
8 SAGE LEAVES
4 SLICES PROSCIUTTO
SALT AND BLACK PEPPER

Lay the cutlets out on a plate. Top each cutlet with two sage leaves and a slice of prosciutto, and press down on them gently. Season the veal lightly with salt (the prosciutto is already salty enough) and pepper. Fry or grill the schnitzels ham-side down to avoid drying out the delicate meat. A few seconds before they are done, flip and briefly fry or grill them on the other side. If you use a frying pan to cook the schnitzels, you can add a tablespoon of butter to the pan. If you have toothpicks, use them to hold the schnitzels together.

Risotto, pasta, salad, or quick ratatouille (page 134) are always good to serve with schnitzels.

TIP:
Try some variations. For example, use chicken (pounded thin)
or firm-fleshed fish, like pickerel or monkfish, instead of the veal cutlets.

For a unique VEGETARIAN version, I top slices of feta or halloumi cheese
with sage leaves. As a substitute for ham, you can use a very thin slice of eggplant,
and a sprinkling of Hungarian paprika for seasoning.

OSSO BUCO WITH GREMOLATA

This dish is a breeze to make in a Dutch oven (page 189).

2 CARROTS
¼ OF A CELERY ROOT
OR 1 CELERY STALK
1 ONION
2 GARLIC CLOVES
2 PIECES OSSO BUCO
(BONE-IN BEEF OR VEAL SHANK),
EACH 12–14 OZ (350–400 G)
2 TBSP ALL-PURPOSE FLOUR
3 TBSP CANOLA OIL
1–2 TBSP TOMATO PASTE
1 CUP (250 ML) ORGANIC VEGETABLE
STOCK OR BEEF BROTH
¾ CUP (200 ML) RED OR WHITE WINE
14 OZ (400 G) CHOPPED CANNED TOMATOES
2 TBSP EACH FRESH ROSEMARY AND THYME
SALT AND BLACK PEPPER

GREMOLATA
1 GARLIC CLOVE
1 ORGANIC LEMON
½ BUNCH PARSLEY

Dice the carrots, celery and onion. Finely chop the garlic. Season the meat with salt and pepper, and dredge each piece in flour. In a Dutch oven or a large heavy pot, heat the oil. Add the meat to the pot and brown well on all sides. Remove meat from the pot and set aside, but do not clean out the pot. Add the vegetables to the remaining oil, and sauté them. Add the tomato paste, the stock or broth, and the wine, and stir. Add the chopped tomatoes. Season generously to taste with salt and pepper. Stir well, scraping along the bottom of the pot as you do so. Return the meat to the pot and place on top of the vegetables. Cover the pot and cook at the edge of the fire or over a low heat. Simmer for 1½ hours. When the meat is practically falling off the bones and very tender, pick the rosemary and thyme leaves from the sprigs and chop them finely. Add the chopped herbs to the braised shanks and stir. If you like, you can mash some of the vegetables with a fork.

To make the gremolata, peel and chop the garlic clove. Wash the lemon in hot water and zest it. Pick the parsley leaves from the stems and finely chop them. Mix all ingredients together.

I love this simple mixture. It also goes well with grilled fish, steak, and so many other dishes, and gives everything a lovely, fresh Mediterranean flavor.

Sprinkle the gremolata over the osso buco (it means "bones with holes" in Italian) and serve the dish with polenta (page 139), mashed potatoes, or fresh bread.

CAMPFIRE BREAD
ON A STICK

MAKES 6–8

⅔ CUP (150 G) SOUR CREAM OR QUARK,
IF AVAILABLE
3 TBSP MILK
5 TBSP CANOLA OIL
1 EGG
10 OZ (300 G) (ABOUT 2 CUPS)
ALL-PURPOSE FLOUR
3 TSP BAKING POWDER
¼ TSP SALT
CHOPPED ROSEMARY,
PESTO OR DIPS (OPTIONAL)

To assemble, divide the dough into 6–8 pieces. Using your fingers, stretch each piece of dough into a long sausage. Take a stick about 3 ft (1m) long, and wrap the dough in a spiral around one end of the stick. Carefully bake the bannock over the campfire or the hot embers. Keep turning the stick slowly until the bread is golden brown on the outside. Enjoy the bread on its own, with grilled food, with pesto (page 27), or with a dip (pages 86–87).

To make a SWEET VERSION of the bread, replace the salt with cinnamon and sugar.

FISH GRILLED ON A STICK

Fish grilled on a stick is known as "steckerlfisch" in my native Upper Bavaria. To make it, a well-seasoned fresh fish is speared onto a thin green branch and grilled over hot coals until the skin is crispy and the fish is cooked. The fish most commonly used for this dish are arctic char or trout. Mackerels are often used in beer gardens and at Oktoberfest. The important thing is to use fish on the fatty side, otherwise it runs the risk of drying out when grilled.

2 FRESH FISH, 7–9 OZ (200–250 G) EACH,
SUCH AS TROUT OR MACKEREL

MARINADE
½ ORGANIC LEMON
6 TBSP OLIVE OIL
1 GARLIC CLOVE
1 SPRIG EACH ROSEMARY, THYME,
AND OREGANO
PINCH OF CHILI POWDER
SALT AND BLACK PEPPER
PINCH OF HUNGARIAN PAPRIKA (OPTIONAL)

To make the marinade, wash the lemon in hot water, zest it, then juice one half of it. In a bowl, whisk the zest, juice, and olive oil. Finley chop or mince the garlic, then add it to the bowl. Pick the rosemary, thyme, and oregano leaves off their stems, chop, and add to the marinade. Season to taste with salt, pepper, chili, and paprika, if using.

Rinse the fish well and pat dry with paper towels. Brush the marinade over the outside of the fish and inside the cavity. This is best done the day before, or in the morning just after you have purchased the fish at the market. Keep the fish in the refrigerator! To grill the fish, insert a fresh, sharpened and debarked hazelnut or willow tree branch (about 2 ft/60 cm long) through the mouth of each fish to the tail end. Alternatively, you also can use very long (!) metal skewers. Place the fish over hot coals or at the edge of the campfire. Turning often, grill until the skin is crispy. Be careful with the heat, otherwise the fish will be charred on the outside but still raw on the inside. If they look dry, brush the fish with marinade every now and then. When the fins on the belly or the spine peel easily away from the flesh, the fish are done.

TIP:
These fish pair perfectly with farmers' bread or a pretzel.
Potato salad or a green salad would also make good accompaniments.

POPCORN

I learned about this marvelously simple way of making camp popcorn in Peru, where it was part of our campfire experience every evening. A Dutch oven (page 189) is perfect for making popcorn.

SALTY

¼ CUP POPPING CORN
2 TBSP CANOLA OIL
2 TBSP SUGAR OR ¼ TSP SALT

Make a campfire. Place your cooking grate over it, and heat the Dutch oven or a large pot until very hot. Remove the pot from the heat. Add the canola oil and the salt or sugar. Sprinkle the corn kernels into the pot, stir briefly, and cover immediately with a lid. Return the pot to the fire. Shake the covered pot now and then.

When you no longer hear any popping sounds, remove the pot from the heat. Pour the the popcorn into a bowl, and let it stand briefly so the steam can escape. This ensures the popcorn will stay nice and crunchy.

SWEET

SWEET LOVE

SWEETS AND DESSERTS

It's magic hour. The day fades away; your body rhythms start to relax.
A perfect outdoor meal deserves to end on a similarly perfect note—a heavenly
dessert, ideally with friends, in your own private restaurant. This
chapter will provide you with exactly the right recipes. They are quick, delicious,
and practically foolproof, whether you make them outdoors or at home.
Your campsite neighbors will be flocking to your van!

PEACH BUNDLES

BAKED APPLES

BAKED PEACHES

BAKED CHOCOLATE
BANANAS

BAKED APPLES FILLED WITH DRIED FRUIT

You can adjust the filling of the apples to suit your taste.
Not just a healthy dessert, baked apples also make a good side
to accompany venison or fowl.

4 TART APPLES,
SUCH AS GALA,
BOSKOOP, OR COX,
IF AVAILABLE
2 TBSP SLIVERED ALMONDS
2 TBSP HONEY
4 TBSP ASSORTED DRIED FRUITS
½ TSP CINNAMON
2 TSP RUM (OPTIONAL)
UNSALTED BUTTER

Wash, but do not peel, the apples. Cut out lids (about ¾ in/2 cm wide) from the top of each apple. Using a sharp knife or an apple corer, core the apples, taking care not to pierce the bottoms. In a dry skillet, toast the slivered almonds until they just start to color. In a bowl, combine the almonds, honey, dried fruit, cinnamon, and rum, if using. Spoon the filling into each apple, packing it in well. Top with a teaspoon of butter (or more as needed), and cover each apple with its lid. Wrap each apple in aluminum foil. Place the apples on the edge of the fire, and bake for 15-20 minutes.

PEACH BUNDLES WITH AMARETTI COOKIE FILLING

If you are making these at home or have an ice cream shop nearby,
they are delicious served à la mode with vanilla or walnut ice cream.

1 TBSP CHOPPED ALMONDS
2 RIPE BUT STILL FIRM PEACHES
2 TBSP AMARETTI COOKIES
OR ALMOND COOKIES
1 TBSP HONEY
1 TBSP RUM (OPTIONAL)

In a dry skillet, toast the almonds until they just start to color. Cut the peaches in half, remove pits, and drizzle with honey and rum, if using.

Coarsely crumble the cookies and combine them with the almonds. Fill the peach halves with the mixture. Wrap each half separately in aluminum foil and grill, skin-side down, for about 10 minutes.

BANANAS BAKED
WITH CHOCOLATE

This is a real flavor explosion! I came across a slightly different version in Asia, where they bake bananas in their skins, then peel them and pour sweetened condensed milk over them. A more decadent but utterly tasty variation, too!

---

2 RIPE BUT STILL FIRM BANANAS
2 BARS DARK CHOCOLATE

Peel off a strip of the banana peel about 1 in (3 cm) wide. Using a knife, cut the inside of the banana into slices 1-1½ in (3-4 cm) thick, making sure not to cut through the banana peel. Press a square of chocolate between each slice of banana.

Wrap the bananas in aluminum foil and bake them, cut-side up, for about 10 minutes.

BAKED PEACHES WITH
ROSEMARY AND HONEY

---

2 RIPE BUT STILL FIRM PEACHES
1 SMALL SPRIG ROSEMARY
3 TBSP HONEY
2 TBSP PINE NUTS
1 CUP PLAIN CHILLED YOGURT

Cut the peaches in half and remove the pits. Pick the rosemary needles off the sprig and finely chop them. Put them in a bowl and mix in 2 tablespoons of the honey. Add the peaches to the bowl cut-side down, and let marinate for about 10 minutes. Meanwhile, in a dry skillet, lightly toast the pine nuts. Put the yogurt in a bowl, add the remaining tablespoon of honey, and mix until smooth. Drain the peaches and reserve the honey marinade. Place a piece of aluminum foil on the grate over the campfire or charcoal. Transfer peaches to the foil and grill for about 2 minutes on each side. Lay the peach halves on a plate, cut-side up, drizzle with honey marinade, and sprinkle with toasted pine nuts. Serve with the chilled yogurt on the side.

TIP:
You can refine this recipe by adding 1 tablespoon of rum to the marinade.

CAMPGROUND
TIRAMISU

This is one of my favorite desserts to make on the road.
It's classic, delicious, and deceptively simple!

¾ CUP MASCARPONE
ABOUT 4 TBSP MILK
2 TBSP BROWN SUGAR
½ ORGANIC LEMON
8 LADYFINGERS
2 SHOTS ESPRESSO
COCOA POWDER

In a bowl, combine the mascarpone, milk, and sugar, and mix until smooth. Wash the lemon in hot water, zest it, and juice it. Add the zest and juice to the mascarpone mixture and combine. In a cup, pour both shots of espresso. Briefly dip each ladyfinger cookie halfway into the coffee. (Depending on their size or shape, you may have to shorten the cookies.) Divide the moistened ladyfingers between two large wide glass jars or dessert bowls, sugar-side down. Pour half of the mascarpone cream over them and smooth the top. Add a second layer of coffee-soaked ladyfingers, pour the remaining mascarpone cream on top, and smooth. Refrigerate the tiramisu for at least 30 minutes. Sprinkle with the cocoa powder, and serve.

You can also prepare the tiramisu in a storage container and serve it straight from there.

TIP:
If you have Kahlúa or another kind of coffee liqueur at home,
take some along in a small jar. Soak the fingers in the Kahlúa then the espresso.
The tiramisu will taste even more irresistible.

CANTUCCINI COOKIES
WITH MASCARPONE CREAM

I adore layered desserts. They rescue us when
unexpected visitors drop in, or if friends spontaneously turn up
at our camper van. Given the versatility of the ingredients,
you can quickly find something that works at a nearby store.

SERVES 4

¾ CUP MASCARPONE
¾ CUP PLAIN GREEK YOGURT
1 TSP PURE VANILLA EXTRACT
ABOUT 16 CANTUCCINI COOKIES
½ GLASS ORANGE JUICE
1 CUP FRESH BERRIES
GRANULATED SUGAR (OPTIONAL)
1–2 TBSP AMARETTO (OPTIONAL)
1 TBSP GRATED CHOCOLATE (OPTIONAL)

In a bowl, place the mascarpone, yogurt, and vanilla extract, and mix to combine. Fold in the grated chocolate, if using.

By hand, break the cookies into pieces (or put them in a freezer bag and crush them roughly with a stone).

Transfer cookie pieces to a bowl, and pour the orange juice and the amaretto, if using, over them. Layer 4 small glass jars with cookies, about 2 tablespoons of mascarpone cream, and berries sprinkled with sugar, if using. Add a second layer of cookies, the remaining mascarpone cream, and a few berries.

Top with grated chocolate, if desired.

TIP:
If you can't source cantuccini cookies or almond biscotti,
use other dry cookies instead, such as butter or almond cookies. You can substitute
sour cream or cream cheese for the mascarpone, but you may need to mix
in 2 teaspoons of milk or cream. And you can replace the berries with bite-sized
pieces of other fresh fruit to suit your taste.

SWEET COUSCOUS WITH DRIED APRICOTS

4 PITTED DATES
4 DRIED SOFT APRICOTS
2 TBSP RAISINS
1 CUP COUSCOUS
PINCH OF SALT
1 TBSP UNSALTED BUTTER
2 TBSP ORANGE JUICE
2 TBSP HONEY
½ TSP CINNAMON
2 TBSP SLICED ALMONDS

Chop the dates and the apricots. Place them in a medium saucepan, add the raisins and couscous, and mix. Pour in boiling water according to the package instructions, add the salt and the butter, and stir briefly. Cover and let stand until all the liquid is absorbed, about 5-10 minutes.

Meanwhile, in a dry skillet, toast the almonds. When the couscous is done, add in the orange juice, honey, and cinnamon, and fluff with a fork. Top the couscous with toasted almonds and serve.

TIP:

This fruity dessert couscous can be tweaked to serve as an exotic side dish with kebabs (page 180), grilled lamb, or chicken. To do so, reduce the honey to 1 tablespoon and season to taste with more salt.

SEMOLINA PUDDING

This creamy dessert is a true classic in Germany, one that brings back warm childhood memories. It is also very practical for the outdoors: lightning-quick, energy-dense, and, of course, delicious.

2 ½ CUPS MILK (ABOUT 500 ML)
3 TBSP BROWN SUGAR, HONEY, OR AGAVE SYRUP
5 TBSP SEMOLINA FLOUR

In a medium saucepan, add the milk and the sugar, honey, or agave syrup, and bring to a soft boil, stirring constantly. Keep stirring and slowly pour in the semolina flour. Simmer briefly, remove from the heat, and let stand for 5 minutes, stirring every now and then.

TIPS FOR PEPPING UP YOUR PUDDING

Sprinkle with cinnamon sugar (ah, the memories!).
Stir in 1 teaspoon Nutella and top with slices of banana.
Top with 1 tablespoon of your favorite jam.
Drizzle with chai syrup (page 28) and sprinkle with chopped nuts.
Serve the pudding with plenty of fresh strawberries.

RICE PUDDING WITH MANGO MINT SALSA

½ CUP COCONUT MILK
½ CUP WATER
PINCH OF SALT
1 CUP SHORT-GRAIN WHITE RICE
2 TBSP BROWN SUGAR OR HONEY
2 TBSP SHREDDED COCONUT
½ FINELY GRATED TONKA BEAN
OR THE SEEDS OF ½ VANILLA BEAN
(OPTIONAL)
1 MANGO
1 SPRIG MINT
1 LIME

In a pot, combine the coconut milk, water, salt, and rice, and bring to a boil. Reduce heat to the lowest setting and cook for about 25 minutes, stirring from time to time. When the rice is done, remove from heat and mix in the sugar and the coconut. Add the tonka or vanilla, if using, and let cool.

Meanwhile, peel and dice the mango. Cut the mint leaves into thin ribbons, reserving some for garnish, and juice the lime. In a bowl, combine the mango, mint, and lime juice and let stand. Arrange the salsa on small plates or around the bottom of small bowls. Spoon the rice pudding over it, garnish with mint, and serve.

TIP:
Put the cooked rice in a moistened scoop or cup, pack it tightly, then invert it over the salsa.

IMPERIAL PANCAKES

Imperial or royal? That is the question. If you have two mixing bowls and some extra time to devote, go the imperial route and beat the egg whites separately for a lighter, airier pancake. Or, put together the royal version—simpler, but no less mouthwatering—and spend that extra time licking your fingers.

¾ CUP ALL-PURPOSE FLOUR
2 CUPS MILK
2–3 EGGS
1 TSP PURE VANILLA EXTRACT
4 TBSP SUGAR
ZEST OF ½ ORGANIC ORANGE OR LEMON
4 TBSP RAISINS
2 TBSP RUM
PINCH OF SALT
1 TBSP NEUTRAL VEGETABLE OIL,
SUCH AS SUNFLOWER
2 TBSP UNSALTED BUTTER
SLIVERED ALMONDS OR OTHER
CHOPPED NUTS (OPTIONAL)
1 TBSP CONFECTIONER'S SUGAR

Separate the eggs. In a large bowl, add the flour with a little bit of milk and whisk until smooth, to prevent the flour from clumping. Whisk in the remaining milk, the egg yolks, vanilla extract, 1 tablespoon of the sugar, the lemon zest, the rum, and the raisins.
In a second, clean bowl, add the egg whites, a pinch of salt, and another tablespoon of the sugar. Beat the egg whites until stiff and glossy. This works with a whisk using a bit of muscle-power, or with an old-fashioned rotary hand mixer. I inherited one from my grandmother; it's an ingenious piece of equipment to have in a camping van. Carefully fold the egg whites into the batter. In a large skillet, heat the oil and 1 tablespoon of the butter over low heat. Gently pour the batter into the skillet to form one large pancake. When the pancake is golden brown on the bottom, cut it into quarters. If the top of the pancake is uncooked, don't fret—just flip the pieces and cook them on the other side. Now things get serious. Using two wooden cooking spoons, tear the quartered pancake into bite-sized pieces. Add the remaining tablespoon of butter along with the remaining 2 tablespoons of sugar. Turn the heat up to medium and caramelize the pancake pieces. Just before removing the pancake pieces, add the almonds to quickly brown. Sprinkle with confectioner's sugar, and serve.

TIP:

Cranberries or caramelized plum compote (page 31) go really well with these.
If you are near an ice cream shop, add a scoop of vanilla ice cream, too!

For the simpler "royal" version, whisk the flour with a little bit of
milk until smooth. Whisk in the remaining milk, the eggs, vanilla extract, 2 tablespoons
of the sugar, lemon zest, rum, raisins, and a pinch of salt. Proceed with cooking the
pancake as detailed above, in the basic recipe. You can also make an apple or pear version
by simply adding diced apple or pear to the batter.

QUICK STRAWBERRY FOOL ⏳ 🪶 🍃

1 CUP FULL-FAT SOUR CREAM
(OR QUARK WITH 20% FAT, IF AVAILABLE)
3 TBSP MILK
1 TSP PURE VANILLA EXTRACT OR
2 TBSP HOMEMADE VANILLA SUGAR (SEE "TIP")
9 OZ (250 G) STRAWBERRIES
2 TBSP HONEY OR BROWN SUGAR
FRESH MINT LEAVES
1 TBSP LEMON JUICE

Place the sour cream or quark in a bowl. Add the milk and vanilla extract or vanilla sugar and mix until smooth. Hull the strawberries, cut them into pieces, and sweeten them with honey or sugar. Carefully fold the strawberries into the sour cream mixture. Add mint and lemon juice as desired.

TIP
HOMEMADE VANILLA SUGAR
When you scrape out the seeds from vanilla beans at home, stick the empty pods into a glass jar or can full of sugar. The more pods you add, the more intense the vanilla flavor will be. Add more sugar and pods as needed, and shake the jar or can to immerse the pods in the sugar. Remove any dried-out pods.

PANCAKES WITH SOUR CREAM TOPPING 🔥 ⏳

PANCAKES
1 CUP ALL-PURPOSE FLOUR
1 TBSP SUGAR
2 TSP BAKING POWDER
PINCH OF SALT
1 EGG
¾ CUP MILK
2 TBSP VEGETABLE OIL PLUS
EXTRA FOR FRYING

In a bowl, mix the flour, sugar, baking powder, and salt. In a separate bowl, whisk the egg with the milk and the oil, then add it to the flour mixture. Working quickly, mix until smooth. Heat more oil in a skillet or pan over medium heat. For each pancake, drop 2 tablespoons of batter into the pan. When light brown on the bottom, flip and cook the pancakes briefly on the other side.

TOPPING
½ ORGANIC ORANGE
¾ CUP SOUR CREAM
1 TBSP HONEY, AGAVE SYRUP,
OR MAPLE SYRUP

For the topping, zest the orange and combine with the sour cream and honey or other sweetener. Add a dollop over the pancakes and serve.

VARIATION
You can omit the sour cream altogether and just go with the classic: Maple syrup, and lots of it!

TIP
If you can get fresh blueberries, add them to the batter before cooking.

SOUTH TYROLEAN BERRY DONUTS

These donuts are called "Krapfen" in South Tyrol, where they serve a dual purpose as both a typical flour-based entree as well as a heavenly dessert. The batter is thinned to make "Strauben," a fried treat you may also know as funnel cake. At village festivals they deep-fry strauben in huge pans, and the deliciously comforting aroma of frying donuts penetrates every lane in the village.

7 OZ (200 G) DAY-OLD WHITE BREAD OR BREAD ROLLS
2 CUPS MILK
2 EGGS
1 ½ CUPS (150 G) ALL-PURPOSE FLOUR
3 ½ OZ (100 G) BLUEBERRIES AND/OR RED CURRANTS OR BLACK CURRANTS
VEGETABLE OIL FOR FRYING, SUCH AS PEANUT OIL
CONFECTIONER'S SUGAR

Cut the bread into rough pieces. In a saucepan, heat the milk. Add the bread and soak for 10 minutes.

In a bowl, whisk the eggs. Squeeze the soaked bread to remove excess milk, and add it to the eggs. Add in the flour then the berries. Mix to make a smooth batter, being careful not to crush the berries.

Fill a pot with about 2 inches of oil. Heat the oil to deep-frying temperature, between 360 °F (180 °C) and 375 °F (190 °C). Be careful, the scalding oil can spatter! Add the batter to the pot one spoonful at a time, and fry until golden brown. Drain the donuts on paper towels.

Dust the donuts with plenty of confectioner's sugar, and enjoy while still warm.

VARIATION

At least once, you must try adding pieces of stone fruit or coarsely chopped elderflower heads to the donut batter!

ROCK CLIMBING

THE VERTICAL DIMENSION

Rock climbing—what an enormous feeling of freedom, so real and so pure. Climbing is a moving meditation in a surreal vertical world suspended between earth and sky. In our rule-driven, protected daily reality, long climbing trips offer a lot of room to make decisions of one's own; decisions rife with consequences. The vertical world is a place in which to retreat. A place where time seems to stand still. The absolute focus on the here and now magnetizes and fascinates most climbers. But between the epic adventure of a long Alpine climbing trip and one's first tentative steps on the rocks, there is now enough room for everyone. Nowadays, there are climbing gyms where you can learn rope techniques, anchoring, how to lead climb on rock, even how to fall.

MARKUS BENDLER

A hot summer's day in Tyrol. I am in a relaxed mood when I meet up with the three-time ice climbing world champion Markus Bendler to do some rock climbing. A likeable, modest Tyrolean in his early thirties, Markus has been climbing for over twenty years. At just fifteen, he was the youngest person in the world to have climbed an 8b+/c (UIAA X) route, one of the hardest grades in rock climbing at the time. This was a real milestone in climbing history. Later on, his ice climbing expeditions took him to faraway places, among others to Iceland and Japan, where he gained a lot of attention by being the first, again, to successfully climb very hard routes.

In competitions he was always a top contender for the title; among other distinctions, he won three world championships. He has since retired from competing, and now just climbs for himself. Now Markus is a "soul-mover." With a great deal of passion, he runs his own climbing shop not far from Kitzbuehel, in Tyrol. If you happen to be in the area, drop by his Rock'n'Roll Mountain Store. Personally-tailored advice, top equipment, and entertaining stories are guaranteed. Markus has many a humorous experience to recount. The climbing trips he goes on are too hard for me, and this gives him a reason to poke fun at me. But who cares! The important thing is being outdoors, so I took this opportunity to find out more about Markus's outdoor life.

ICE CLIMBING IS VERY ATHLETIC, AND THE TRAINING IS INTENSE. HOW MANY DAYS A YEAR DID YOU SPEND ON THE ROCKS AND ICE DURING YOUR COMPETITION DAYS?

During my competition phase, I was outside climbing five days a week on average. Sometimes I also trained twice a day.

WHEN YOU SET OFF ON ONE OF YOUR LONGER EXPEDITIONS, ASIDE FROM YOUR CLIMBING GEAR, WHAT DID YOU ALWAYS HAVE IN YOUR LUGGAGE?

Food! Whether I was going on a climbing expedition or traveling to compete, I always took along cheese, sausages (usually smoked sausages, smoked bacon, and smoked dry sausages), bread, mustard, and horseradish. This ensured my survival as a little Tyrolean out in the big wide world!

WHAT WAS YOUR FUNNIEST MOMENT IN THE MOUNTAINS?

It's actually always very funny when I'm on the road with my buddies, so it's hard to pick just one moment. Depending on our mood, we often use dialects that we have acquired over the years. So we can spend days speaking in the dialects of the Ziller Valley, Oetzt Valley, South Tyrol, Switzerland, Franconia, or Swabia. People have asked me what part of Franconia I come from.

AND NOW TO GET SERIOUS... WERE YOU EVER IN A TRICKY SITUATION ON A MOUNTAIN WHICH, ULTIMATELY, ENDED WELL? DID THIS INFLUENCE YOU LATER ON?

A climbing partner—and good friend— once made an oversight tying two ropes together and was a hair's breadth away from falling. Luckily, an instant before disaster struck, I noticed the mistake and firmly held on to both my friend and the rope. Since then I check every knot twice.

AND FINALLY, OF COURSE: WHAT'S YOUR FAVORITE POWER FOOD ON THE ROCKS AND ICE? AND WHAT'S YOUR FAVORITE MEAL FOR RECHARGING AT HOME?

When I'm climbing my diet is rather unhealthy; a ham sandwich, granola bars, Snickers bars, water, a Coke from time to time. At home I usually cook spaghetti carbonara or steak with salad and potatoes. In summertime, we also regularly barbecue outdoors.

REFRESH

THIRST-QUENCHERS AND WAKE-UP DRINKS

Good hydration is important. After a long day outdoors, and certainly
after doing sports, proper hydration replenishes lost electrolytes,
speeds up recovery, and helps prevent cramps and injuries. The perfect post-sport
drink in my book is a passion fruit shandy. "But wait," you may say. "I'm not
sporty!" No worries—the recipes that follow are not just for the athletes among us.
They are perfect also on a lazy afternoon, when the sun disappears behind
the mountains, or when the ocean shimmers against a fiery evening sky. These drinks
will quench your thirst, wake you up, or help you send off the day.
Enjoy, and cheers!

CAMP COFFEE

Camping without coffee? Only in an emergency. For most people,
coffee is an enjoyable drink; but it is also an essential drink, even when
you are on the move. It can be an Italian cappuccino or a simple
affair, like coffee made in an enamel pot over the campfire; it doesn't
matter. A caffeinated camper is a happy camper.

For great coffee every time, here's a rundown of all the
ways to prepare coffee and the types of vessels used.

FILTER COFFEE

Filter (or drip) coffee is not just for retro fans. In hip Scandinavian coffee bars, drip coffee has made a comeback. Set the filter brewer on almost any heatproof pot. Place a paper coffee filter inside and add ground coffee. Pour a tiny amount of boiling water over the coffee to saturate the grounds. Give it about 30 seconds, then pour more boiling water and stop. Repeat until you have the desired amount of coffee in the pot. As a rule, use 1 heaping teaspoon of coffee per cup of water.

PERCOLATOR COFFEE

Another blast from the past, percolators are often enameled, and are as equally well-suited to the open fire as they are to the home stove. A coffee basket is mounted on a metal stem inside the pot. As the water boils, the percolator brews and gurgles and produces coffee automatically. It's perfect for campfire romantics!

TURKISH COFFEE

This is the absolute oldest method of preparing coffee worldwide. Strong and black with a Middle-Eastern flair, the coffee is ground super-finely and brewed in an *ibrik*, a small metal pot with a long handle. Stir together one small cup cold water, 1 heaping teaspoon coffee, and 1 teaspoon of sugar. Heat the water slowly until it foams. Remove from heat briefly; stir, then return the pot to the heat and let it foam a second time. Pour the coffee into demitasse or espresso cups and wait a bit for the grounds to settle. Drink the coffee black, but do not drink the dregs!

ESPRESSO COFFEE

Whether you use an iconic Bialetti or any other moka pot, this stovetop espresso maker also uses the percolating principle to brew consistently good coffee. Moka pots are made of aluminum or stainless steel; I prefer, and recommend, stainless steel. If using an aluminum moka pot, clean it only with water, and never put it in the dishwasher. To use, fill the strainer with ground coffee up to just below the top. Don't pack the coffee down. Pour water up to the bottom of the overflow valve. Assemble the pot, making sure the rubber gasket is properly sealed and not damaged, place it over medium heat, and let it bubble away!

If you have room, pack a small milk frother so you can enjoy a creamy cappuccino or latte wherever, whenever.

FRENCH PRESS COFFEE

Many manufacturers, such as Bodum, make their French press coffee makers out of glass, which I would not recommend for camping. If you have a more robust stainless steel one (made by KitchenAid, for example), then definitely take that along in the camper van. Just as with Turkish coffee, there is no need for a filter. Add the ground coffee to the pot then pour in hot water. Use about 4 tablespoons of ground coffee for every 2 cups of water. Let steep for 3-4 minutes, plunge the filter down, and enjoy the coffee straightaway.

CHAI LATTE

2 CUPS MILK
6 TBSP CHAI SYRUP
(PAGE 28)

Warm the milk gently until you can only just hold your finger in it. Don't let it boil! Using a whisk or a handheld milk frother, beat the milk until it is creamy and foamy. Add 3 tablespoons of chai syrup to each mug or tall glass, and top with the foamed milk. (Alternatively, if you have a jug-style milk frother, use it to heat and froth the milk at the same time.)

To give your chai latte some extra oomph, add a shot of espresso to each mug or glass.

PASSION FRUIT SHANDY

2 TSP LIME SYRUP
2 TSP LEMON JUICE
¼ CUP PASSION FRUIT JUICE
2 CUPS NON-ALCOHOLIC WHEAT BEER

Pour the beer into a pitcher. Stir together the syrup, lemon juice, and passion fruit juice, and add to the pitcher.

TIP
If you don't have any lime syrup, make your own:
fill a shot glass with lime juice,
add ½ tablespoon brown sugar, and stir.

GINGER BEER

½ CUP (100 ML) GINGER SYRUP
(PAGE 28)
3 CUPS SPARKLING MINERAL WATER
4 SLICES ORGANIC LEMON

Add ice cubes, if you have them, to four glasses. Divide the syrup and the sparkling water between the glasses, and garnish with lemon slices.

FERMENTED GINGER BEER

3 CUPS MINERAL WATER
4 TBSP BROWN SUGAR
THUMB OF FRESH GINGER
(ABOUT 1 INCH LONG)
1 ORGANIC LEMON
1 ORGANIC ORANGE
¼ TSP INSTANT YEAST

Combine the water and the sugar and boil to make simple syrup. Grate the ginger into the syrup. Wash the orange and the lemon in hot water. Juice the lemon; zest and juice the orange. Add the zest and juices to the syrup. When the syrup is lukewarm, stir in the yeast.

Pour the liquid into a bottle that holds 4 ¼ cups (1L), but do not cap it. Let the liquid ferment at room temperature for about two days, then strain the ginger beer and refrigerate.

BUS PUNCH

This makes a wonderful, refreshing fruity drink for balmy summer evenings. Sip it barefoot on the beach, as you relax on a picnic blanket in tall grass with music playing... or as you sit in front of your camper van savoring the moment.

4 RIPE NECTARINES OR
1 CONTAINER RASPBERRIES
¼ SMALL WATERMELON
2 TBSP BROWN SUGAR
1 CUP ORANGE JUICE
1 BOTTLE LIGHT ROSÉ WINE, IDEALLY CHILLED

Wash, pit, and cube the nectarines. Cut away the rind from the watermelon and cube the flesh, removing as many seeds as you can. Put the fruit in a bowl. Add the sugar and the orange juice, stir, and let steep. Just before serving, pour in the chilled wine.

VIRGIN MOJITO

2 ORGANIC LIMES
2 SPRIGS FRESH MINT
2 TSP BROWN SUGAR
1½ CUPS (330 ML) GINGER ALE
2 TSP ELDERFLOWER SYRUP (PAGE 28)
CRUSHED ICE, IF AVAILABLE

Wash the limes and roll them over a cutting board, using gentle pressure, to help extract more juice. Cut each lime into 8 wedges. Pick the mint leaves from the stems. Divide the lime wedges between two large glasses. Add the sugar. Crush the lime wedges using the handle of a cooking spoon, and stir. Add the elderflower syrup and ice cubes, if available, pour in the ginger ale, and stir again. For the authentic experience, drink the mojito with a straw.

LEMONADES

An idyllic flashback to childhood, homemade lemonades are hip again. These refreshing and fruity thirst-quenchers are quick to prepare and can be made with ingredients that are readily available. Even so, they never fail to impress.

GREEN APPLE LEMONADE

1 SMALL GREEN APPLE
2 ORGANIC LIMES
4 SPRIGS LEMON BALM OR MINT
3–4 CUPS TONIC WATER
ICE CUBES, IF AVAILABLE

Wash, core, and thinly slice the apple. Wash the limes and cut them in half. Juice the 3 lime halves, and thinly slice the fourth. Pick the lemon balm or mint leaves from their stems. Place all ingredients in a pitcher, stir, and serve-with ice cubes, if possible.

REFRESHING ICED TEA

4 CUPS WATER
2 TEA BAGS BLACK TEA,
SUCH AS DARJEELING
3 SPRIGS FRESH MINT
1½ ORGANIC LEMON
6–8 TBSP ELDERFLOWER
SYRUP (PAGE 28)
ICE CUBES

In a pot, bring the water to a boil. Add the tea bags and the mint, and let steep for 3 minutes. Remove the tea bags. Add the juice of 1 lemon and the elderflower syrup to the pot. Slice the remaining half lemon and add to the pot. Let cool, and serve with plenty of ice cubes.

Alternatively, if you don't have any syrup on hand, you can sweeten the tea with 4–6 teaspoons of brown sugar. If you don't have any fresh mint, you can use a peppermint tea bag instead.

This iced tea tastes surprisingly refreshing when it is warm, too!

TIP
Plan ahead: brew the tea at home, and fish out the mint leaves along with the tea bags. When the tea has cooled, fill plastic bottles three-quarters of the way full and freeze them. The bottles make excellent cooler packs for your cooler bag, and later, of course, double as iced tea. To serve, just add a few slices of lemon.

PINK GRAPEFRUIT LEMONADE

2 CUPS FRESHLY-SQUEEZED
PINK GRAPEFRUIT JUICE
½ CUP FRESHLY-SQUEEZED LEMON JUICE
3 TBSP BROWN SUGAR
2 CUPS SPARKLING MINERAL WATER
ORGANIC LIME OR LEMON SLICES
ICE CUBES, IF AVAILABLE

Place the sugar and the juices in a pitcher. Pour in the sparkling water and stir. Add ice cubes if you have them, and garnish with lime or lemon slices.

APPLE PUNCH

1 ORGANIC LEMON
¾ OZ (20 G) FRESH GINGER
2 WHOLE CLOVES
2 CUPS APPLE JUICE
1 TSP BROWN SUGAR
1 CINNAMON STICK
OR ¼ TSP CINNAMON POWDER
SEEDS OF ½ VANILLA BEAN

Wash the lemon in hot water. Zest it,
cut it in half, and juice one of the halves.
Peel and chop the ginger and coarsely
crush the clove buds.

In a pot, place all ingredients except
the lemon juice. Heat the liquid slowly,
stirring until the sugar has dissolved.
Stir in the lemon juice. Strain the punch
through a fine-mesh sieve and serve hot.

TIP
If you would like to spike your punch,
add a bit of Amaretto or Calvados.

YOU
CAN'T
GIVE
YOUR
LIFE
MORE
TIME,
SO
GIVE
THE
TIME
YOU
HAVE
LEFT
MORE
LIFE.

RECIPE INDEX

AT HOME

Apricot and coconut
power balls 41
Basic pesto 26
Beetroot pesto 27
Berry booster granola 35
Breakfast porridge 34
Burger buns 25
Caramelized plum compote 31
Chai syrup 28
Elderflower syrup 28
Fig and nut power balls 40
Funky fruit granola 35
Ginger syrup 28
Macadamia monster trail mix 39
Monkey munch trail mix 38
Pesto Genovese 27
Power push trail mix 39
Rhubarb syrup 28
Squash cookies 36
Strawberry and rhubarb jam 31
Sun-dried tomato pesto 27
Trail bars 37
Tyrolean nut cakes baked in
jars 32
Wild garlic pesto 27

DINING IN

Asian stir-fry with millet and
vegetables 144
Ceviche 119
Chickpea curry 129
Hearty lentil stew with bacon
and potatoes 121
Mie goreng 133
Minestrone 135
Moroccan salad with tomatoes
and cucumber 114
Mushroom polenta 139

Penne with tuna and olives 116
Portuguese fish stew 125
Quick ratatouille 134
Red wine polenta 139
Risotto 138
Saffron polenta 139
Spaghetti Bolognese 117
Spinach and cheese
dumplings 140
Sweet polenta 139
Thai curry with rice 128
Truffled polenta 139
Wild rice and mango salad 130
White bean stew with Italian
sausage 120

DINING OUT

Adana kebab 180
Bacon cheeseburger 166
Baked potatoes with herbed
fresh cheese 185
Baked vegetables with
Feta cheese 185
Big Italian burger 169
Big Kahuna burger 169
Campfire bread on a stick 200
Chicken satay 180
Cod fillets with an
oat crust 175
Fire barrel cheese fondue 178
Fish grilled on a stick 203
Flatbread grilled on
a stone 180
Fried sweet potatoes with
asparagus 183
Italian antipasti
vegetables 160
Lamb shawarma 182
Mediterranean chicken stew 187
Osso buco with gremolata 198
Popcorn 204

Saltimbocca—Italian veal
schnitzels 194
Tagliata—Italian sliced
steak 172
Veggie burger 169
Whole fish from the grill 192

QUICK REFUEL

Avocado dip 87
Bruschetta with tomato and
basil 81
Caesar salad 76
Club tortilla wrap 91
Crostini 81
Falafel 84
Funky tuna sandwich 90
Goat cheese quesadilla 96
Greek-style quesadilla 96
Hummus 86
Orange and fennel salad with
Feta cheese 77
Panzanella—classic Tuscan
bread and tomato salad 75
Perfect tomato salad 80
Quick spaghetti carbonara with
avocado 94
Quinoa salad 79
Super fast spaghetti
carbonara 94
Tabouleh 78
Tortilla española 97
Tuna dip 87
Tyrolean farmers' hash 99
Yogurt-lemon dip 87

REFRESH

Apple punch 259
Camper van punch 251
Chai latte 247

Ginger beer 248
Green apple lemonade 252
Passion fruit shandy 248
Pink grapefruit lemonade 255
Refreshing iced tea 255
Virgin mojito 251

Savory pancakes with cottage
cheese filling 62
Super fried eggs 54
Super granola 46
Rice pudding 48
Western breakfast 56

SWEET LOVE

Baked apples filled with dried
fruit 215
Baked Chocolate bananas 216
Baked peaches with rosemary
and honey 216
Campground tiramisu 219
Cantuccini cookies layered with
mascarpone cream 221
Imperial pancakes 225
Pancakes with sour cream
topping 229
Peach bundles with amaretti
cookie filling 215
Quick strawberry fool 229
Rice pudding with mango mint
salsa 223
Semolina pudding 222
South Tyrolean berry
donuts 231
Sweet couscous with dried
apricots 222

MISCELLANEOUS

Always on board—packing
checklists 23
Bouldering—a creative and
free way of moving 64
Camp coffee 244
Cutting an onion—how to do
it the right way 83
Dutch oven 189
Hiking—relaxing outdoor
meditation 103
How to fillet a fish 176
How to know if a fish is
fresh 193
Light my fire—campfire
tips 158
Mountain biking—pure flow 147
My dream mountain Alpamayo—
excerpts from my Peru
expedition journal 50
Outdoor eating at its best 89
Rock climbing—the vertical
dimension 233

WAKE-UP CALL

Andean Breakfast
with quinoa 49
Four minute tea eggs 55
Morning munch—the ultimate
sandwich 61
Overnight oats 47
Porridge with bananas 47
Power frittata with oats 60

GENERAL INDEX

Adana kebab 180
amaretti
  Peach bundles with amaretti
  cookie filling 215
Andean breakfast with
quinoa 49
apples
  Apple punch 259
  Baked apples filled with
  dried fruit 215
  Green apple lemonade 252
apricots
  Apricot and coconut power
  balls 41
  Sweet couscous with dried
  apricots 222
Asian stir-fry with millet
and vegetables 144
asparagus
  Fried sweet potatoes with
  asparagus 183
avocados
  Avocado dip 87
  Caesar salad 76
  Morning munch—the ultimate
  sandwich 61
  Quick spaghetti carbonara
  with avocado 94
bacon
  Bacon cheeseburger 166
  Hearty lentil stew with bacon
  and potatoes 121
  Tyrolean farmers' hash 99
  Western breakfast 56
baked beans
  Baked apples filled with
  dried fruit 215
  Baked chocolate bananas 216
  Baked peaches with rosemary
  and honey 216
  Baked potatoes with herbed
  fresh cheese 185
  Western breakfast 56
bananas
  Baked chocolate bananas 216

Porridge with bananas 47
beans
  White bean stew with
  Italian sausage 120
beef
  Osso buco with gremolata 198
  Tagliata—Italian sliced
  steak 172
beetroot
  Beetroot pesto 27
berries
  Berry booster granola 35
  Quick strawberry fool 229
  South Tyrolean berry
  donuts 231
Big Italian burger 169
Big Kahuna burger 169
bread
  Bruschetta with tomato and
  basil 81
  Crostini 81
  Funky tuna sandwich 90
  Morning munch—the ultimate
  sandwich 61
  Panzanella—classic Tuscan
  bread and tomato salad 75
Breakfast porridge 34
bruschetta
  Bruschetta with tomato and
  basil 81
cakes
  Tyrolean nut cakes baked in
  jars 32
cantuccini
  Cantuccini cookies layered
  with mascarpone cream 221
Caramelized plum compote 31
carbonara
  Quick spaghetti carbonara
  with avocado 94
  Super fast spaghetti
  carbonara 94
Ceviche 119
Chai latte 247
Chai syrup 28

Cheeseburger 166
cheese
  Fire barrel cheese fondue 178
  Spinach and cheese
  dumplings 140
chicken
  Caesar salad 76
  Chicken satay 180
  Club tortilla wrap 91
  Mediterranean chicken
  stew 187
  Thai curry with rice 128
chickpeas
  Chickpea curry 129
  Falafel 84
  Hummus 86
chocolate
  Baked chocolate bananas 216
cocktails
  Virgin mojito 251
coconut
  Apricot and coconut power
  balls 41
  Coconut milk
  Thai curry with rice 128
Cod fillets with an oat
crust 175
cookies
  Squash cookies 36
cottage cheese
  Savory pancakes with cottage
  cheese filling 62
couscous
  Sweet couscous with dried
  apricots 222
Crostini 81
cucumber
  Moroccan salad with tomatoes
  and cucumber 114
curry
  Chickpea curry 129
  Thai curry with rice 128
dips
  Avocado dip 87
  Hummus 86

Tuna dip 87
Yogurt-lemon dip 87
donuts
    South Tyrolean berry
    donuts 231
dried fruit
    Baked apples filled with
    dried fruit 215
dumplings
    Spinach and cheese
    dumplings 140
eggs
    Four minute tea eggs 55
    Quick spaghetti carbonara
    with avocado 94
    Super fast spaghetti
    carbonara 94
    Super fried eggs 54
    Tortilla española 97
    Tyrolean farmers' hash 99
    Western breakfast 56
elderflower
    Elderflower syrup 28
falafel
    Falafel 84
    Veggie burger 169
fennel
    Orange and fennel salad with
Feta cheese 77
Fermented ginger beer 248
feta cheese
    Baked vegetables with Feta
    cheese 185
    Fire barrel cheese fondue 178
    Orange and fennel salad with
    Feta cheese 77
Fig and nut power balls 40
fish
    Ceviche 119
    Cod fillets with an oat
    crust 175
    Fish grilled on a stick 203
    Portuguese fish stew 125
    Whole fish from
    the grill 192

Flatbread grilled on
a stone 180
Four minute tea eggs 55
Fried sweet potatoes with
asparagus 183
Funky fruit granola 35
Funky tuna sandwich 90
ginger
    Ginger beer 248
    Ginger syrup 28
granola
    Super granola 46
granola trail mixes
    Berry booster granola 35
    Funky fruit granola 35
granola trail bars
    Trail bars 37
grapefruit
    Green apple lemonade 252
    Pink grapefruit lemonade 255
gremolata
    Osso buco with gremolata 198
ground beef
    Adana kebab 180
    Bacon cheeseburger 166
    Big Italian burger 169
    Big Kahuna burger 169
    Spaghetti Bolognese 117
Hearty lentil stew with bacon
and potatoes 121
Hummus 86
iced tea
    Refreshing iced tea 255
Imperial pancakes 225
Italian antipasti
vegetables 160
Italian sausage
    White bean stew with Italian
    sausage 120
Lamb shawarma 182
lemonade
    Green apple lemonade 252
    Pink grapefruit lemonade 255
lemons
    Yogurt-lemon dip 87

lentils
    Hearty lentil stew with bacon
    and potatoes 121
limes
    Ceviche 119
Macadamia monster trail mix 39
mango
    Rice pudding with mango mint
    salsa 223
Mediterranean chicken stew 187
Mie goreng 133
millet
    Asian stir-fry with millet
    and vegetables 144
Minestrone 135
mint
    Rice pudding with mango mint
    salsa 223
Monkey munch trail mix 38
Moroccan salad with tomatoes
and cucumber 114
Mushroom polenta 139
nectarines
    Camper van punch 251
nuts
    Fig and nut power
    balls 40
    Tyrolean nut cakes baked
    in jars 32
oats
    Breakfast porridge 34
    Cod fillets with an oat
    crust 175
    Overnight oats 47
    Power frittata with oats 60
olives
    Penne with tuna and
    olives 116
omelet
    Power frittata with oats 60
    Tortilla española 97
Orange and fennel salad with
Feta cheese 77
Osso buco with gremolata 198
Overnight oats 47

pancakes
   Pancakes with sour cream
   topping 229
   Savory pancakes with cottage
   cheese filling 62
Panzanella—classic Tuscan
bread and tomato salad 75
Passion fruit shandy 248
pasta
   Penne with tuna and
   olives 116
   Quick spaghetti carbonara
   with avocado 94
   Spaghetti Bolognese 117
   Super fast spaghetti
   carbonara 94
peaches
   Baked peaches with rosemary
   and honey 216
   Peach bundles with amaretti
   cookie filling 215
Penne with tuna and olives 116
pesto
   basic pesto 26
   Beetroot pesto 27
   Pesto Genovese 27
   Sun-dried tomato pesto 27
   Wild garlic pesto 27
Picnics 89
Pink grapefruit lemonade 255
plums
   Caramelized plum compote 31
polenta
   Mushroom polenta 139
   Red wine polenta 139
   Saffron polenta 139
   Sweet polenta 139
   Truffled polenta 139
Popcorn 204
potatoes
   Baked potatoes with herbed
   fresh cheese 185
   Hearty lentil stew with bacon
   and potatoes 121
   Tortilla española 97

Tyrolean farmers' hash 99
porridge
   Breakfast porridge 34
   Porridge with bananas 47
Portuguese fish stew 125
power balls
   Apricot and coconut
   power balls 41
   Fig and nut power balls 40
Power frittata with oats 60
Power push trail mix 39
punch
   Apple punch 259
quark
   Baked potatoes with herbed
   fresh cheese 185
   Quick strawberry fool 229
quesadilla
   Goat cheese quesadilla 96
   Greek-style quesadilla 96
Quick ratatouille 134
Quick spaghetti carbonara with
avocado 94
Quick strawberry fool 229
quinoa
   Andean breakfast with
   quinoa 49
   Quinoa salad 79
raspberries
   Camper van punch 251
ratatouille
   Quick ratatouille 134
Risotto 138
Red wine polenta 139
Refreshing iced tea 255
rhubarb
   Rhubarb syrup 28
   Strawberry and rhubarb jam 31
Rice
   Rice pudding 48
   Rice pudding with mango
   mint salsa 223
   Thai curry with rice 128
   Wild rice and mango salad 130
Rice pudding 48

Rosé wine
   Camper van punch 251
Saffron polenta 139
salads
   Caesar salad 76
   Moroccan salad with tomatoes
   and cucumber 114
   Orange and fennel salad with
   Feta cheese 77
   Panzanella—classic
   Tuscan bread and tomato
   salad 75
   Perfect tomato salad 80
   Quinoa salad 79
   Tabouleh 78
   Wild rice and mango salad 130
Saltimbocca—Italian veal
schnitzels 194
sandwiches
   Funky tuna sandwich 90
   Morning munch—the ultimate
   sandwich 61
Savory pancakes with cottage
cheese filling 62
Sausage
   White bean stew with Italian
   sausage 120
schnitzels
   Saltimbocca—Italian veal
   schnitzels 194
Semolina pudding 222
skewers
   Adana kebab 180
   Chicken satay 180
soup
   Minestrone 135
spaghetti
   Quick spaghetti carbonara
   with avocado 94
   Spaghetti Bolognese 117
   Super-fast spaghetti
   carbonara 94
Spinach and cheese
dumplings 140
Squash cookies 36

steak
   Tagliata—Italian sliced
   steak 172
stews
   Hearty lentil stew with bacon
   and potatoes 121
   Mediterranean chicken
   stew 187
   Portuguese fish stew 125
   White bean stew with
   Italian sausage 120
strawberries
   Quick strawberry fool 229
   Strawberry and rhubarb
   jam 31
Super fried eggs 54
Super granola 46
Sweet couscous with dried
apricots 222
sweet potatoes
   Fried sweet potatoes with
   asparagus 183
   Western breakfast 56
syrups
   Chai syrup 28
   Elderflower syrup 28
   Ginger beer 248
   Ginger syrup 28
   Passion fruit shandy 248
   Refreshing iced tea 255
   Rhubarb syrup 28
Tabouleh 78
Tagliata—Italian sliced
steak 172
tea
   Four minute tea eggs 55
   Refreshing iced tea 255
Thai curry with rice 128
tiramisu
   Campground tiramisu 219
tomatoes
   Moroccan salad with tomatoes
   and cucumber 114
   Morning munch—the ultimate
   sandwich 61

Panzanella—classic
Tuscan bread and tomato
salad 75
   Perfect tomato salad 80
Tortilla española 97
tortillas
   Club tortilla wrap 91
   Fresh goat quesadilla 96
   Greek-style quesadilla 96
trail mixes
   Macadamia monster trail
   mix 39
   Monkey munch trail mix 38
   Power push trail mix 39
Trail bars 37
Truffeled polenta 139
tuna
   Funky tuna sandwich 90
   Penne with tuna and
   olives 116
   Tuna dip 87
Tyrolean farmers' hash 99
Tyrolean nut cakes baked in
jars 32
Veal
   Osso buco with gremolata 198
   Saltimbocca—Italian veal
   schnitzels 194
vegetables
   Asian stir-fry with millet
   and vegetables 144
   Baked vegetables with Feta
   cheese 185
   Italian antipasti
   vegetables 160
Veggie burger 169
Virgin mojito 251
Watermelon camper van punch 251
Western breakfast 56
Whole fish from the grill 192
Wild garlic pesto 27
Wild rice and mango salad 130
Wraps
   Club tortilla wrap 91
Yogurt-lemon dip 87

SPECIAL THANKS

This book took over a year to complete, and now it is behind me.
It was a long path from the first presentation at the publisher's to the print version.
Along this path, I was supported by many friends and family—thank you. I would also like to give
big thanks to Vanessa and Angela of Umschau Verlag. Thank you for always being there,
for your support, and for the fact that you never lost sight of the big picture.

Anne Fischer, for the emotional support and your consulting and marketing work.

Armin Schmidt (Frischmarkt Schondorf and others), for his generous support in providing the
best local food products for our food photography.

Our models, friends, and helpers: Vicky, Martin, Matheo, Bianca, Michi, Lukas Gerum
and Markus Reiser of Focus Bikepark in Oberammergau, Heike, Stacy, Sophie, and Markus Bendler.

We would like to thank Maloja and Globetrotter for the close and personal work we enjoyed
together, and for their active support.

maloja   **Globetrotter**
<< NEUE HORIZONTE >>

The GREAT OUTDOORS

120 RECIPES FOR ADVENTURE COOKING

by Markus Sämmer

Translation by Barbara Hopkinson

Project Management by Cyra Pfennings

Art Direction and Design by C100/Christian Hundertmark
Layout by Mona Osterkamp and Stefan Morgner

Lifestyle, Outdoor, and Sport Photography by Steffen Schulte-Lippern
Food Photography by Peter Greppmayr

Illustration by Florian Bayer (pages 20–21)

Typefaces: Aperçu by The Entente, Modern Love by Giuseppe Salerno and Paco González,
Renovation by Veneta Rangelova, Noteworthy by Emily Spadoni, Typewriter by Volker Busse

Edited by Robert Klanten

Printed by Nino Druck GmbH, Neustadt/Weinstraße
Made in Germany

Published by Gestalten, Berlin 2018
ISBN 978-3-89955-948-4

First published in 2017 under the title of
THE GREAT OUTDOORS—120 GENIALE RAUSZEIT-REZEPTE by Neuer Umschau Buchverlag GmbH,
Im Altenschemel 21, 67435 Neustadt/Weinstraße, Germany.

For more information, please visit www.gestalten.com.

Bibliographic information published by the Deutsche Nationalbibliothek.
The Deutsche Nationalbibliothek lists this publication in the Deutsche Nationalbibliografie;
detailed bibliographic data are available online at http://dnb.d-nb.de.

This book was printed on paper certified according to the standards of the FSC®.

MIX
Paper from
responsible sources
FSC® C006655